How to teach
and manage
children with
ADHD

WITHDRAWN

Fintan J O'Regan

Fintan J O'Regan is currently the Headteacher of the Centre Academy in London, which is
recognised as the first established school and assessment centre in the UK for the diagnosis,
teaching and management of ADHD and/or related learning difficulties.
Having studied Genetics/Zoology at the University of Sheffield and a PGCE at Newcastle University,
he taught in the North East for a number of years before joining the Washington DC International
High School in USA.
He joined the Centre Academy in 1988 and has been directly involved in both the teaching and
management of ADHD/Dyslexic students during this period, becoming Headteacher in 1997. He
completed a Master's degree in Educational Management in 1996.
Fintan has given lectures and workshops on ADHD throughout the UK and Ireland, both to
professionals and parents, and has appeared on a number of TV and radio shows on the subject. In
addition, he has written a number of published articles and is the author of *Educating Children
with ADHD*, published in June, 2001.
Formerly the Vice Chairman of the Corporate Members of the British Dyslexia Association, he sits
on the London International Schools Association, and is involved with the National Association of
Special Needs and a number of ADHD parent support groups.
Fintan has been married to Sue for 10 years. They have a daughter Kendal aged 5, twins Brennan
and Connor aged 3, and a very interesting cat named Kossof.

How to teach and manage children with ADHD
LL01527
ISBN 18 5503 348 8
© Fintan J O'Regan
Cover illustration by Peter Wilks
Inside illustrations by Rebecca Barnes
All rights reserved
First published 2002
Reprinted 2002, 2003, 2004

Printed in the UK for LDA
LDA, Duke Street, Wisbech, Cambs PE13 2AE
3195 Wilson Drive, Grand Rapids, MI 49544, USA

Contents

Contents

Preface

Preface

This book provides information about the ADHD learning style and ideas for the proactive management of pupils affected by ADHD. It is divided into five chapters.

Chapter 1 gives a short introduction to the nature of ADHD and its impact on the child in school.

Chapter 2 moves on to the key management principles – structure, differentiation, flexibility and relationships – that can help you plan and succeed. This chapter examines the role of the teacher, individual subjects and the thorny issue of homework.

Chapter 3 considers socialisation issues, highlighting the differences in management of boys and girls. It looks at how unstructured times, like break time, affect students with ADHD. Sports and field trips are also considered.

Chapter 4 looks at how other professionals impact on the student's life.

Chapter 5 provides some samples of ideas, resources and materials.

In the Appendix the sources for this book are listed.

The main aim of this book is to empower you to help those with ADHD by informing you about the condition. We also hope to promote a process of thinking about strategies that enable pupils with ADHD to gain full access to the curriculum, and become successful and happy students.

I'd like to say thanks to a number of people for their help with this book. Firstly, to Susie, my wife, for everlasting support and to the 'squids' – Kendal, Brennan and Connor – for putting off trips to the park on Sunday afternoons so I could work on this book. In addition, thanks to my editor, Lee Humber, the ever-patient and encouraging force in this project. Finally, last but not least, to all the students and staff that I have worked with over the years, without whom none of this would have been possible.

Acronyms

The following acronyms are used in this book.

ADHD	Attention Deficit Hyperactivity Disorder
CD	Conduct Disorder
CT	Combined Type
DfES	Department for Education and Skills
DSMIV	*Diagnostic and Statistical Manual of the American Psychiatric Association*
DT	Design Technology
EBD	Emotional and Behavioural Difficulties
FT	Food Technology
HIT	Hyperactive Impulsive Type
IEP	Individual Education Plan
NICE	National Council for Clinical Excellence
NQT	Non-Qualified Teacher
ODD	Oppositional Defiant Disorder
PIT	Predominantly Inattentive Type
PSHE	Personal, Social and Health Education
SEN	Special Educational Needs
SENCo	Special Educational Needs Co-ordinator
SpLD	Specific Learning Difficulties
TOAD	Talk out of turn, Out of seat, Attention, Disrupt

'Ian can do it when he wants to'

'Paul is inattentive'

'Susie has problems finishing and starting work'

'Danny always disturbs others'

'Dew's handwriting is awful'

'Tania has lack of self-control

'She is always off task'

'Mickey is always on the go'

'Chloe is driven by a motor'

'Andy is volatile'

'David has problems changing from one task to another'

'Tom is restless all the time'

'Wayne is indifferent to rewards and punishments'

'Scott is easily bored'

'Sadie is always seeking attention'

'Bev is so difficult to get started in the morning'

Chapter 1
Teaching Children
with ADHD

ADHD explained

If you recognise all, some or any of the character traits presented on the facing page, then it is time to consider the precise nature of the condition that may be causing them.

The term Attention Deficit Hyperactivity Disorder (ADHD) originates from the fourth edition of the *Diagnostic and Statistical Manual of the American Psychiatric Association,* 1994 (referred to as DSMIV). It is the most recent version of a medical diagnosis that has changed considerably since it was first proposed as a distinct medical condition by the English paediatrician George Still in 1902. In the UK until recently, the term 'hyperkinetic disorder' (see Diagnostic criteria section on page 60) has more often been applied, using guidelines laid down by the International Classification of Diseases in 1992. That term describes a similar population of children to those now covered by the broader ADHD category.

The DSMIV lists three ADHD types:

○ Predominantly Inattentive Type (PIT)
○ Hyperactive Impulsive Type (HIT)
○ Combined Type (CT).

Types of student

The key features of the ADHD diagnosis are inattention, hyperactivity and impulsivity, each of which may be defined more fully. The behavioural characteristics, based on DSMIV, are as follows.

Inattention
○ Often fails to give close attention to detail or makes careless mistakes in schoolwork, work or other activities.
○ Often has difficulty sustaining attention in tasks or play activities.
○ Easily distracted from tasks and play activities.
○ Often does not seem to listen when spoken to directly.
○ Often does not follow instructions through and fails to finish schoolwork, jobs or duties in the workplace (not owing to oppositional behaviour or failure to understand instructions).
○ Often has difficulty in organising tasks and activities.
○ Often avoids, dislikes or is reluctant to engage in tasks that require sustained

mental effort (such as schoolwork or homework).

○ Often loses things necessary for tasks or activities (e.g. toys, schoolwork, pencils, books or tools).

○ Is often forgetful in daily activities.

Hyperactivity

○ Often fidgets with hands or feet or squirms in seat.

○ Leaves seat in classroom or in other situations in which remaining seated is expected.

○ Often runs about or climbs in situations in which these are inappropriate (in adolescents or adults this may be limited to subjective feelings of restlessness).

○ Often has difficulty in playing or engaging in leisure activities quietly.

○ Is often 'on the go' or acts as if driven by a motor.

○ Often talks excessively.

Impulsivity

○ Often blurts out answers before questions have been completed.

○ Often has difficulty in waiting for a turn.

○ Often interrupts or intrudes on others (e.g. butts into conversations or games).

Every one of us occasionally displays some or all of these characteristics. In mainstream classrooms, at some time most children will behave in some of these ways when stressed, tired, bored or just 'not in the mood'. They may be unable to concentrate and may become distracted, excited, agitated or anxious. Impulsive, fidgety or restless behaviour may follow. Children (and adults) may also display some or all of these behaviours when they are ill. If these features persistently occur and illness or stress is ruled out then the possibility of ADHD must be considered.

For the ADHD diagnosis to be made the following conditions must be met:

○ The number and type of symptoms should be consistent with the conditions laid down in the diagnostic criteria. The child must display six or more of the symptoms from the inattention list (PIT) beginning on page 7, or six or more from the combined hyperactivity and impulsivity lists (HIT) above.

○ The problems must have persisted for at least six months to a degree that is maladaptive and inconsistent with the child's developmental level.

○ There must be evidence that some of these symptoms were present before the age of 7 years.

○ Problems are pervasive across two or more settings, for example at school (or work) and at home.

○ There must be clear evidence of clinically significant impairment in social, academic or occupational functioning (i.e. the symptoms must interfere significantly with the individual's emotional, educational or professional functioning).

○ The symptoms are not directly related to a pervasive developmental disorder, schizophrenia or other psychotic disorder, and are not better accounted for by another mental disorder (as described in the DSMIV, e.g. mood disorder, anxiety disorder, dissociative disorder or personality disorder).

To be diagnosed as CT (Combined Type) children will have six or more symptoms from both the PIT and HIT lists.

It is more difficult for a child to meet the criteria for hyperkinetic disorder than for ADHD. There are two reasons for this. Firstly, the child must meet the criteria for CT ADHD. Secondly, the professional making the diagnosis must observe the relevant behaviours at first hand.

Using different criteria to identify ADHD is a problem that affects deciding on the correct treatment of the individuals concerned. It is to be hoped that UK and European professionals will accept DSMIV in the near future as the main basis for classification.

How many people are affected?

Worldwide between 1 and 6 per cent of the school-age population is estimated to be affected by ADHD, according to the most reliable figures, which were presented by R. Tannock in his paper, 'ADHD: Advantages in Cognitive Neurobiological and Genetic Research', *Journal of Child Psychology and Psychiatry*, 39(1), 65. It is thought that:

① boys outnumber girls 4:1 in the HIT group;
② boys and girls are represented in about equal numbers in the PIT group;
③ approximately 80 per cent of students with ADHD are behind in at least one academic subject;
④ approximately 25 per cent of students with ADHD will be expelled from secondary school owing to serious misconduct.

In the USA, the most commonly agreed estimates for the population as a whole are that ADHD affects around 3 to 5 per cent of all North Americans and 5 to 7 per cent of school-age children.

In the UK it has been estimated that 1.8 per cent of children experience hyperkinetic disorder and that these are a subgroup of the approximately 5 per cent of school-age children who have ADHD. This means that in the UK there will be, on average, one or two children with ADHD in every single classroom. Because of the impact of the child with ADHD on the classroom environment, all children and teachers across the country are potentially affected directly or indirectly by the condition.

The only consistent feature of the ADHD child is their inconsistency

The ADHD diagnosis cannot be applied to any child who appears naughty, or difficult, or has a tendency to daydream. It is also wrong to apply the ADHD label to children who may be suffering from emotional and behavioural difficulties (EBD). In the year 2000, according to the organisation Young Minds, between 10 and 20 per cent of the school population of England and Wales were children with EBD. If we are to diagnose ADHD, symptoms must be persistent, pervasive and noticed at an early age. Even applying these strict criteria, it is evident that the condition affects a substantial minority of school students.

The inconsistency of behaviour of the child with ADHD puzzles and frustrates parents, teachers and schoolmates alike. On occasion, the child with ADHD may be attentive to a task and may not be impulsive or hyperactive. This creates the impression that the child's usual inability to sustain attention or control their impulses is a wilful act indicating laziness and lack of motivation. This interpretation misses the point. A central problem for children with ADHD is sustaining a consistent level of performance in schoolwork and other activities. Many of the incidental sights and sounds that most children are able to ignore are highly intrusive to the child with ADHD. Responding to the sound of a chair being scraped on the floor or another child coughing often causes the child with ADHD to be accused of deliberately avoiding completing a task.

New interpretations

Although ADHD is a term that is largely accepted in the UK and the USA, new ideas continually impact on it. Russell Barkley has recently proposed a condition called 'behavioural inhibition' in his book *ADHD and the Nature of Self-Control* (1997). This builds on the ideas that individuals are unable to stop themselves responding to specific stimuli. Barkley also suggests that ADHD children have poor short-term or working memories. This would mean the child has limited ability to manage time.

The working memory is the area of the brain in which we hold information to monitor time and manipulate the sequence of events. If students are deficient in this area, they will be attracted to more interesting activities than monitoring time. In any specific period concentration will be focused on areas of direct interest only and all others will be ignored.

An illustration of this would be the child playing on a computer whose mother tells them they have minutes left to get ready for school. Given the limitations of their working memory, the chances that they are going to allocate enough resources to monitoring that time are very slim. As a result the mother will think the child has not paid attention or has ignored the request. Either way they are likely to end up in trouble because of their failure to follow the instruction.

Case Study

Nine-year-old Martin, fidgeting in his seat, was having a bad day. His name was already on the board and the lesson was only ten minutes old. How was he going to survive the next 40 minutes? The lesson was history and Martin liked history. He liked all the stuff about wars, fighting and castles. Things in the past seemed so much more interesting than now. The teacher asked a question and Martin knew the answer. Straightaway he burst out of his seat, his hand pumping furiously, desperate to get the answer out. His teacher ignored him and asked another child.

Martin slumped back into his chair, totally exasperated. The child who had been asked the question got the answer wrong and so did another child who was asked. The teacher turned to Martin and said, 'Do you know the answer to the question, Martin? You had your hand up.'

Martin, fiddling with his pencil, said quickly, 'What question, Miss?'

For Martin the moment had passed. Previously he had the answer, but later he could not remember the question.

Looking at working memory as a cause of learning difficulties is not new. Studies into the causes of dyslexia point to deficiencies in this region of the brain as a possible explanation.

There is a huge overlap between ADHD and other learning difficulties, including dyslexia, dyspraxia, Asperger's, giftedness and EBD. Two other conditions found in the DSMIV – Conduct Disorder (CD) and Oppositional Defiant Disorder (ODD) – often appear either to coincide with or even mask ADHD. (Criteria for these are listed in the Diagnostic criteria section, pages 60 and 61.)

Although we shall not look at these in detail, the overall management of all students with non-traditional learning styles will need to be taken into account. Secondary or co-existing learning or behavioural issues almost always exist or develop alongside ADHD.

Another View

I have found it useful to divide students with ADHD into three groups:

Attention Defiant Disorder
This type is the oppositional angry student who doesn't care any more as the whole world is against them. They have developed a cocoon around themselves. Over the years this barrier will become a thicker defensive wall to protect them from the comments of teachers and parents. From this self-centred fortress spats and temper tantrums may be launched if they are challenged over the smallest issue.

Attention Detachment Disorder
This type is the completely lethargic 'space cadet' student. Passive resistance has replaced defiance. Many of these students have effectively given up. This student is completely unresponsive to positive or negative reinforcement and has opted out of trying to achieve or attempt educational or social targets.

Attention Dizzy Disorder
This type is the bright and breezy student whose attitude and zest for life remains undiminished despite their problems at school or at home. These children may have had a more understanding framework and remain positive in their attitude and enthusiastic in their hyperactive and impulsive learning style. It is unlikely that they will remain this way for long. Given the pressures of traditional schooling, it is likely to be only a matter of time before they evolve into one of the types listed above.

It is essential to look at children with ADHD, not ADHD children. There is a subtle difference but a key one. We must focus on the children themselves and we need to depersonalise the symptoms. One way for teachers to reframe the situation is to view children with ADHD as 'computers without their printers attached'. Often these children have all the information in their heads but cannot get it down onto paper. Today having your thoughts down on paper in hard-copy form is what counts. Without the ability for the printer to be attached, the thoughts and intelligence of the child will drift off into cyberspace. Meanwhile, books remain empty, marks are poor and frustrations build – leading to failure

*'If you think
education is
expensive try
ignorance'
Derek Bok*

and loss of self-confidence.

It has been said, 'Time is a state of thinking that stops everything from happening together by parcelling moments out into separate bits.' To the ADHD sufferer time becomes a black hole. Everything appears to happen at once, creating a state of inner turmoil and panic in which perspective is lost and problems in relating to others start.

Students with ADHD may be highly imaginative and intuitive, with an impulse to get to the heart of the matter as opposed to taking the traditional methodical approach. It is to the teaching and management of students with ADHD that we therefore now turn.

Case Study

Sarah, aged 6: 'Sometimes, when I wiggle about in my seat and burp, the teacher says it bothers the children near me. She says I do it on purpose and, often, she then sits beside me for a while. She also says no poking others or staring at them as it makes them mad. After this, I have to walk around the room with my hands in my pockets, staring at my feet when I walk ... so then I bump into things and then she gets even madder at me ... I mean I really can't win .... my name is always on the board.'

Chapter 2
Structure, Differentiation, Flexibility and Relationships

'If you think you can, you can, if you think you can't, you're right'
Mary Kay Ash

Four terms – structure, differentiation, flexibility and relationships – are particularly important when developing strategies to teach children with ADHD.

A structure of consistent routine, rules and guidelines forms the basis of all teaching systems. Its importance is even greater for children with ADHD. Differentiation relates to the delivery of the curriculum – in content, style, format, application and quantity. It should be applied both inside and outside the classroom. Both structure and differentiation must be applied with flexibility.

Adaptation of the curriculum applies to all children. For children with ADHD constant revision of curriculum provision is required and needs to be proactively pursued. Underpinning all of the above are the relationships built between the people working with children with ADHD and the children themselves, determining the cohesion with which they can work together.

Teaching staff need to be child centred, strong minded and patient. They need a sense of humour and perspective sufficient to qualify them for sainthood. In addition, they need to be able to work in harness with other professionals and develop an open mind about whether or not they fully trust their contribution. Last, but certainly not least, they need to establish a working relationship with the parents of the children concerned.

Structure and systems

If the key to buying and selling property is 'location, location and location', then the key to teaching children with ADHD is 'structure, structure and structure'. Structure can only be achieved through the consistent application of systems. For children with ADHD 'structure' is one of the most feared words they will encounter. For them, it means torture as it smacks of routine and boredom. However, despite initial fears, children with ADHD will find out that they need it – the trick is how to sell the process to them.

A regular timetable from Monday to Friday with an unchanging pattern of lessons is preferable. Schools with a six-day or two-week timetable provide a difficult but not insurmountable challenge, as long as the system is not altered once the student with ADHD is used to it. Different classes occurring on different days in different rooms with different teachers is the worst situation. Children with ADHD must have a familiar pattern to their day and the more structured and regular the timetable, the better.

Ideally a structured framework should start off with a period every morning when the tasks of the day are outlined by a specific teacher or mentor. The school week should allow for the same subject to be scheduled at the same time each day. Within the classroom each student with ADHD should be assigned to a specific desk. This should be a separate unit, cutting out direct contact with and distraction from other students.

'80 per cent of success is showing up' Woody Allen

Children's storage areas should be located in or near the classroom to help the organisation of books and materials. Where possible, teachers should travel to children. This will allow children to concentrate on their work instead of having to move rooms and pack up all their materials eight or nine times a day.

Creating a specifically structured week may be beyond the scope of most school schedules. If so, then the key elements to manage are changes in whatever routines are established. Events such as the school photograph day, sports day, prize-giving day and so on are guaranteed to take the child with ADHD out of the 'comfort zone' and into the unknown, with resultant fall-out.

Further key areas on which to focus school systems are the following:

① Punctuality.
② Uniform or dress codes.
③ Behavioural systems.
④ Peer/staff relations.

Time-keeping is one area in which little compromise is advisable. Children must learn to be where they need to be on time. If rigid discipline were to apply to only one element of managing ADHD children, then this is it.

Dress code is a less clearly defined area. However, a degree of control by the school over the way students are dressed is another way of creating a structured approach before students come into the classroom. Many battles will be fought between weary teachers and students over this issue, but this will be an early indicator of whether students will conform (or not) to the types of system that the teacher is attempting to enforce.

In tandem with school structure, behavioural systems need to be set up to reflect positive and negative performance. Tokens, stickers, goal charts and certificates are just a few examples.

'Enthusiasm is contagious – and so is the lack of it' Anonymous

Remember, children with ADHD need to be rewarded or disciplined immediately. Long-term goal targets, like earning a good report at the end of the term, will not work. Children need to have immediate, consistent, tangible results like a sticker, a certificate or points for a behavioural system to work. The typical child with ADHD lives in the present. They find it hard to look at the future and have little relationship with the past. Once the moment is past, it really is history – which is one of many reasons why they find it difficult to accept responsibility for their actions.

It can sometimes be difficult to find motivators for children. Sometimes it is just by good luck (or divine intervention) that you find a system that achieves the desired result.

Behaviour systems need to be based on a response–cost relationship in which students either gain or lose rewards in accordance with task completion or behaviour targets.

Case Study

Punctuality in the morning was one of the many issues for Steven, a 16-year-old student who fitted into the PIT category. We ran a system for some older students in which punctuality was rewarded by the privilege of being allowed off campus at lunchtime. Steven never came in on time, so he was never given this privilege and did not leave campus. This was normally a privilege students would give their right arm for. For Steven it didn't work at all – until we discovered why.

We found Steven liked being inside. Being an inattentive, detached sort, Steven didn't mix easily and preferred to be indoors drawing or playing with his laptop alone, not socialising. As a result of our discovery we changed tack. Now, every time he was late we insisted he went off campus at lunchtime. He had to earn the right to stay in.

This worked for a period until the issue of lateness returned. He grew to like going out at lunchtime. We reverted to the original system, which finally solved the problem.

Positive rewards differ according to the age of the student – ranging from extra computer or playtime for younger students to off-campus privileges for older students. One youngster I taught found cleaning out the hamster cage was a motivational reward.

'Take care to get what you like or you'll be forced to like what you get'
George Bernard Shaw

For negative reinforcement there should be a graduated scheme of perhaps 16 to 20 steps, starting with non-verbal teacher response – a stare – and finishing up with exclusion as the ultimate sanction. (See Chapter 5, Support Materials, begining on page 51 for more advice on behaviour management.) In conjunction with this there should be clear and defined academic expectations and fairly rigid penalties for non-completed tasks. However tough or non-compliant a student may appear, all are terribly inconvenienced by having to stay behind after school.

The establishment of specific expectations about how children relate to staff and their peers is all important. Consistency and reasonableness are key features of this. Although teachers will operate different styles of classroom management, a minimum number of definitive rules should apply. For example, there should be strict monitoring of bad language towards staff and pupils. Children should not bring to class anything other than what is needed for the lesson. Mobile phones should be switched off at the beginning of the school day and left off. Children should keep their hands away from other children's personal effects and, of course, there should be no physical contact with other children.

The definitive rules should be simple and limited to five or six in number. Additional secondary guidelines for behaviour and expectations can be introduced, leaving room for flexibility for teachers.

Behaviour systems should always seek the following:

① To develop the philosophy that there are 'no throw-away kids'.

② To find and nurture unique competencies in every child.

③ To teach children how to stop and think before acting.

④ To provide teacher monitoring and reinforcement for completed assignments, appropriate behaviour and conforming to rules.

⑤ To move towards self-monitoring (e.g. the child keeps track of the due dates for assignment completion, appropriate behaviour and conforming to rules.

⑥ To think of alternative solutions for conflict situations and to recognise pitfalls ahead of time.

⑦ To develop a plan to avoid hassle and evaluate the efficiency of the strategy, seeking other solutions if the plan does not work.

Differentiation of subjects

Traditional school teaching systems present many difficulties for children with ADHD. Christopher Green, in his book *Understanding ADHD*, 1997, suggested that up to 50 per cent of these children will have learning problems in reading, spelling, writing, mathematics or language. Many children will underachieve academically owing to the 'double whammy' of ADHD and associated learning problems. Inattention, hyperactivity and impulsivity – combined with difficulties with the mechanics of reading, comprehension, sequencing, visual and auditory processing and poor fine and gross motor skills – are a recipe for academic failure.

As children move on from Key Stage 1, Key Stages 2 and 3 present a wide range of subjects with all students between the ages of 4 and 14 studying up to 16 different subjects per week. Although 14- to 16-year-old students will concentrate on between six and ten subjects, the majority of these will be presented in a standardised 1,330 hours per year chalk-and-talk framework. This must be adapted for students with non-traditional learning styles.

'Education is not so much the filling of a pail but the lighting of a fire'
William Butler Yeats

For children with ADHD the number and variety of subjects strikes at the heart of their lack of organisational skill. This is the fundamental technique all children need to manage their timetable. Other key study skills for consideration include active listening, note taking, problem solving and test taking. Equally important is the acquisition through specific teaching of an understanding of estimation and formulae for maths. In this context differentiation of lessons is essential.

Below we provide an outline of the positive and negative elements of specific subjects for children with ADHD, followed by suggestions for management.

Literacy for younger children

In addition to concentration difficulties, many children with ADHD will have handwriting difficulties. As a result, insisting on neatness and on children re-doing untidy work will only alienate the child from writing. It is better to develop different ways of recording or registering that their work is complete.

For example, ADHD children could draw pictures or diagrams to describe their thoughts. Handwriting should be taught as a separate skill. Spelling is difficult and should also be taught separately from other skills. Two skills should not be taught at once. Use visual aids, such as 5 – 10-minute video presentations, and computers for the same length of time to break up the 60-minute period further. See page 59 in the Support materials chapter for how to break down the Literacy Hour for children with ADHD.

English language for older children
Positives
○ Students typically love writing stories – or at least beginning them – and often say they like *literacy* English (even if they don't do very well at it).
Negatives
○ Lack of comprehension.
○ Spelling and handwriting weaknesses, in terms of poorly developed motor skills.
○ Poor story completion due to loss of interest.

Children often prefer to answer verbally, not write their answers down.

For reading and language the best method of teaching is a structured, cumulative programme. This should be assisted by specific visual, auditory and computer support and, if the child has co-morbid dyslexia or dyspraxic difficulties, with appropriate phonological awareness, visual motor and specialised linguistic support programmes. Writing is a consistent problem and needs a specialised approach which may involve an occupational therapist. Teaching basics like pen grip, letter flow and size constancy are essential. Provide options that do not include writing, for example oral exercises instead of written ones. Children may need to dictate their answers to a scribe.

Assign and expect reasonable quantities of work. Basic spelling skills are important but once a child has a degree of confidence do not be afraid to encourage the use of computer spell-checks.

English literature for older children
Positives
○ Though reading may be a problem, children really do like to lose themselves in the imaginary worlds that good literature creates.
○ Drama is popular with children who like to verbalise and act out their feelings.
Negatives
○ The abstract ideas of poetry and the language of Shakespeare prove difficult.

Discover what works for each child and focus on the strengths, not the weaknesses. Be proactive and creative to stimulate interest. For example, if Shakespeare is required, the Mel Gibson version of *Hamlet* is very accessible, as is the Leonardo DiCaprio version of *Romeo and Juliet*.

Numeracy for younger children
When teaching numeracy to younger children, bear in mind that they will often have poor attention to detail. Mark worksheets with highlighter pens to focus

attention. Children become bored very easily so it is better to work with four work cards with five problems on each, rather than with one work sheet with twenty. Use a 'Maths window' – a small piece of cardboard with a window cut out – which can be used as an overlay on a page of multiple problems. This helps focus attention on a specific problem. Use of appropriate computer software is recommended. See page 59 for suggestions on breaking down the Numeracy hour for children with ADHD.

Numeracy for older children

Positives

○ Students may be quite strong in mathematical reasoning and many enjoy numbers more than letters. This is because many children with ADHD and other learning difficulties have highly developed spatial learning skills and often adapt well to the geometrical aspects of the subject.

Negatives

○ The use of sentences in maths may confuse children.

○ Sequential learning in algebra, long division and fractions all cause problems.

○ Related areas of decimals and percentages may also cause difficulties.

○ There are often significant weaknesses in memory skills, especially for abstract symbols.

○ Being taught different ways to find an answer to a question causes frustration.

Establish what a child's learning style is. Are they an 'inchworm' structured learner or a 'grasshopper' type – many students with ADHD are – who jumps stages in a lateral, interactive approach? Work should be broken up into short segments as boredom sets in easily after a number of questions on a similar topic. Using graph paper instead of notebook paper may be helpful. Allow extra time for tests.

Explain the language of maths. Words like 'linear' and 'extrapolate' are meaningless unless specifically explained. 'Add' may also be expressed as 'plus', 'total' or even 'find the sum of'. If tables are not known, do not dwell on this as that could lower self-esteem. Permit the use of calculators and reinforce mathematical principles on computers.

Science for younger children

For subjects such as science, physical education, design technology and food technology, the key consideration is safety. Children will act first and, maybe, think later. Proactive supervision of activities is best, with the support of a teaching or student assistant. Group the child with ADHD with another child who can demonstrate how to follow instructions.
On the positive side, children with ADHD usually enjoy lessons in which they have the opportunity to be active.

Science for older children

Positives

○ Provides opportunities to use materials and develop manipulation skills. This gets them out of their seats for part of the day. Most children enjoy biology, doing chemistry experiments and topics in physics like light, heat and sound.

Negatives
○ Because of their impulsivity, and often hyperactivity and hypoactivity, experimentation may be dangerous and must be carefully supervised.
○ Some areas to avoid, or differentiate carefully, are chemical equations, molarity in general, mechanics in physics and half-lives in radiation.

There is a complete set of new terms in science, all of which need to be specifically taught. A science vocabulary page should be to hand. Questions need to be specific and clearly in context. For example, if you ask somebody 'What is a base?' in chemistry don't be surprised if the answer is 'The bottom of a building.' This is not a wrong answer, but a response to a poor question.

Use a structured approach to lab reports, comprising title, investigation, materials, apparatus, method, diagram, results, discussion and conclusion. Put two students in each group only. In this case, three really is a crowd.

Information and communication technology

Positives
○ Children appear to be able to adapt well to this multi-sensory, multi-media world. They find computers stimulating, challenging and a medium that can hold their focus. In addition, computers don't yell or have favourites.
○ Children can often control the pace at which they work and appear to like the game approach to learning.

Negatives
○ Computers can crash and the students' response may be aggressive.
○ Software needs to be carefully chosen.
○ Keyboards may be overwhelming if not introduced properly.
○ Touch-typing instruction is an absolute requirement for all.

Computers are a useful tool but not a substitute for good teaching practice. Computers should be used to complement most parts of the overall teaching programme, while additional emphasis could be given to specific areas in which severe learning difficulties occur.

'Often the best way to win is to forget to keep the score'
Marianne Espinosa Murphy

Geography and history

Stear clear of a chalk-and-talk approach. Keep verbal presentations short. Short comprehension tasks should be completed during class time and backed up by video presentations.

Art, design technology (DT) and food technology (FT)

Positives
○ These are often the subjects that children with ADHD enjoy the most.

Negatives
○ Many children may have poor gross manipulative skills and fine motor difficulties. These subjects may highlight these physical difficulties.
○ Safety issues need to be carefully considered.
○ It is common in many schools for children who are performing poorly in English or maths to be taken out of art, DT or FT to have extra tuition in the

core subjects. This is a bad mistake and undermines the positive reinforcement generated by the creative freedom of design and cookery.

Modern foreign languages

Positives
o Some students may have an excellent affinity for languages.
Negatives
o The weak concentration skills of many students make this a difficult class.
o Most secondary curriculums include a second language. Language teaching is usually auditory in style, needing good listening and conversation skills.

Be flexible. Keep teaching as visual as possible and use short bursts of auditory work. Be creative in teaching aspects of a different culture – study the French towns with teams that English football clubs play, for example. Try cross-curricular studies with FT or history.

Assemblies

Sitting and listening in large groups for an extended period of time is difficult for children with ADHD. Consider whether the child needs to attend at all. If they do, create time for the child to move around and chatter before the assembly, followed by a calming-down period. Accompany the child to the assembly and provide the child with something to fidget or draw with during assembly.

General teaching tips

① Review material constantly, providing repetition.
② Use humorous mnemonics to assist memorising.
③ Clarify and emphasise important concepts during teaching sessions.
④ Teach definitions and subject-specific terms carefully.
⑤ Extend time limits.
⑥ Break long lessons into easily attainable steps.
⑦ When using the board face students while you speak.
⑧ When evaluating work, emphasise quality or quantity, not both.
⑨ Correct and return written work as quickly as possible.
⑩ Give frequent quizzes.
⑪ Provide students with a detailed course syllabus.
⑫ Select textbooks carefully.
⑬ Teach textbook aids (index, glossary, table of contents).
⑭ Assign readings well in advance.
⑮ Do not yell at children. They hear only the noise, not the message.

'Make the work interesting and the discipline will take care of itself'
E.B. White

Successful multi-sensory teaching can be achieved if we bear in mind the findings of M. Agnew, S. Barlow, L. Pascal and S. Skidmore, published in 1996 in their book *Get Better Grades*: 'We remember 20% of what we read, 30% of what we hear, 40% of what we see, 50% of what we say, 60% of what we do and 90% of what we see, hear, say and do.'

Homework

Homework causes great friction between children, their parents and teachers. For children with ADHD getting the materials home unscathed is a major triumph. At home, settling down to work in an area away from TV, siblings and the outside attractions of the garden, friends and so on is often a major problem. Children who struggle to work in school will find it virtually impossible to achieve consistency in completing work at home.

A weekly student homework assignment sheet – not a diary – is essential. Each task should be written down, checked and signed by a teacher at the end of each lesson for which homework is due. The total assignments provided should be checked again by the form tutor at the end of the day.

For specific students a 60-minute session of homework after school, supervised by staff, may be useful. This encourages students to complete the bulk of their homework before they leave the building. In my own school this system considerably improved the quality and quantity of completed assignments. It also helped raise the self-esteem and confidence of students in what had been a very demoralising part of their education.

When preparing homework be mindful of the following '3 Rs':

Relevance: Assignments should be directly related to classroom work.

Review: All homework assignments should be a review of material previously covered. New or unfamiliar concepts should not be introduced as homework.

Realism: It generally takes an ADHD student three times as long to complete an assignment at home as it would to complete it in a structured classroom setting.

Flexibility in action

Management of the classroom is difficult with any group of students. Class size, subject demands and the range of abilities and types of students are all variables that create problems. Add children with ADHD to the mix and the likelihood of conflict increases substantially. Classrooms need careful management if a long-term relationship between students and teacher is to be built. This calls for a tight structure to be applied with the utmost flexibility.

Discipline and flexibility

Discipline and flexibility may appear to sit uneasily together, but flexible approaches to enforcing discipline do exist. Let us look at a child who refuses to comply with instructions. See whether the child has their own strategy for compliance. Often, the child may not be able to comply because of the way the instruction is given. By adapting discipline to suit their own style, an outcome to suit both parties is achievable. There is a much better chance of successful classroom management if students themselves have been involved in the process. Self-help student problem-solving strategies do have their drawbacks, but as long as the teacher keeps control of the

Food For Thought

Sometimes there are students who are particularly hard nuts to crack. Try singing to them. 'American Pie', by Don McLean, was very effective with Nat, a 15-year-old at my school with attitude and learning difficulties. He was sitting in my office letting off steam and telling me he refused to do the detention he had been given. Listening until he finished, I then began the song and had got only to the second line when, looking at me incredulously, he said, 'What are you doing, Sir?' When I explained I was going to sing to him unless he took his detention he remained defiant. Two verses on and unable to stand any more, he said, 'OK, I'll do it.' As he left I reminded him the song has seven verses and I would be happy to sing him the rest next time he was sent to me.

Playing Country and Western tunes to students seems to have a similar effect!

'To expect to rule others by assuming a loud tone is like thinking oneself tall by putting on high heels'
J. Petit-Seun

overall aims this method of working can be very successful.

Often it is necessary to identify the core problem from within the matrix of observed behaviours. In these cases situational analysis is helpful. This calls for the teacher (or parent if applied in the home environment) to record and note a list of factors that may have contributed to the child's 'bad day'. Factors may include the following:

① Time of day, day of week.
② Temperature.
③ Subject area.
④ Classroom activity.
⑤ Demands of class – e.g. writing down.
⑥ Absentees – e.g. a best friend missing.
⑦ Hunger pangs.

Common factors for which specific plans can be devised may be identified. This may result in revision of the student's schedule and curriculum. It may include making a decision about whether the student attends the class at all. (For more detail, see Chapter 5, Support Materials.)

Verbal confrontation with children must be avoided. The key factor is to try to think beyond the situation at hand. It is the campaign you are trying to win, not every battle. Flexibility in this is strongly advised. It may be difficult. Certain students will 'wind you up' more than others. External and personal factors will affect teacher mood and thereby teacher response in specific situations.

Be honest with yourself. Identify the likely flash points and try to bypass them. Avoid the temptation to 'take him or her on'. Invariably you will lose not just the confrontation but also the respect of other students in the process.

When asking a student to leave the classroom to cool off, a non-verbal system may be more effective than telling them to do so in front of their peers. The secret of surviving adolescence is avoiding embarrassment amongst friends, and certain students will cause major classroom scenes if challenged by the teacher in front of their mates. Non-verbal methods like specific hand signals or even a nod of the head are often more effective than verbal commands.

Here are a number of potential flash-point situations with suggested solutions.

Waiting

Problem
All waiting situations are difficult for children with ADHD. Queuing, waiting for games to begin, for teachers to finish conversations, for others to complete work – all of these may cause stress with resultant behaviour problems.

Solution
○ Limit the amount of waiting time to a minimum wherever possible.
○ Appoint a child who does not have ADHD as a study buddy.
○ Use computers for extra activities.

Short-term memory problems

Problem

Forgetting rules and instructions as soon as these are provided is very common.

Solution

○ Use memory aids. For example, use visual clues to control talking in class – green for go and red for stop.

○ Use daily work schedules checked by each teacher after every lesson.

○ Minimise oral instructions and ask the child to repeat them after you.

○ Teach mnemonics for instructions.

○ Try using cooker timers for timed tasks – these show the available time remaining.

Sitting and concentrating

Problem

Short attention spans make sitting and concentrating very difficult.

Solution

○ Let the child scribble or draw while you are speaking.

○ Let them underline with marker pens.

○ If a child is having problems sitting, allow them to stand up at their desk.

○ Instructions should be 'Turn to page 16, paragraph 4, beginning with the word "Before"', not 'Open your books'.

'A teacher affects eternity; he can never tell where his influence stops'
Henry Adams

Impulsivity (verbal or physical)

Problem

Both verbal and physical impulsivity are common.

Solution

○ Encourage children to write down thoughts and ideas and put them in a box on their desk for later teacher attention.

○ Encourage a stop, wait and count to ten approach.

Classroom becoming stressful

Problem

A child is annoying you and everyone else in the class. The pressure is building.

Solution

○ Be specific with your demands.

○ If you have to respond verbally, make sure you avoid an angry or sarcastic tone. Other children will pick up your attitudes to particular children and will transfer them to their own attitude to the child.

○ Let the disruptive child go to a designated work area and work with headphones on, or to another classroom, to relieve pressure on the group.

The child cannot self-monitor

Problem

Children with ADHD may have difficulty in monitoring their own behaviour.

Solution

○ Reinforce positive behaviour as much as possible. The more often you are positive about particular aspects of a child's behaviour, the more the issue will be reinforced. 'Thank you for raising your hand' is simple but very effective.

○ Let the child know they can signal you when they need to go to their quiet corner or stand outside.

Reward system problems

Problem

Rewards and sanctions work in the short term and but not in the long term.

Solution

○ Have the child help in determining what rewards or sanctions should be applied for positive and negative behaviours. This will help them become less confrontational and improve self-esteem.

Distractions

Problem

The child may have difficulty remaining on task.

Solution

○ Provide access to an independent area away from the rest of the group, and to tasks on computer.

○ Allow headphones to be used. The right music can have a calming and focusing effect.

○ During group work restrict groups to one other pupil only.

A refusal to accept responsibility in a flash-point situation

Problem

The child with ADHD may fail to accept responsibility for their part in tense situations.

Solution

○ Do not force the situation.

○ Do not argue or try to explain.

○ Remove the child from the group and place them in a time-out area where they can vent their frustrations.

○ Talk things through later, with counselling help if need be.

Relationships with staff

All of the people working with students must be willing to adapt their approach to the individual's specific needs. The most important thing for children with ADHD is that they have at least one person with whom they have a positive relationship. That person should act as the advocate for or mentor of the child, and be the person who assesses and addresses the child's academic and socialisation needs. Ideally the mentor would be the class or form teacher. The school counsellor, SENCo, head or deputy head, or a child-centred NQT could also take on the role. Co-ordinating and being able to monitor a consistent approach with all those who come in contact with the child is the key.

Another View

Teachers, like students, come in many forms. Below are a few of my own observations.

The drifter
They drifted into teaching via college because they couldn't think of anything else to do. They liked being a student themselves and wanted to maintain their holiday regime. They love field trips and teacher conferences. Often they maintain strong political leanings.

Born to teach
The vocational teacher, from day one. In their own childhood nursery they lined up all of their stuffed animals and dolls to give them a lecture from the junior blackboard-and-chalk set given to them for their second birthday.

The specialist
The subject specialist loves history or maths and is puzzled by the fact that not everybody else does.

The careerist
The career teacher is learning the ropes only so they can manage other teachers in due course en route for their headship.

Teachers are unlikely to have had any advice or training on how to manage non-traditional learners like children with ADHD. The acid test of a good teacher is how well they respond when they meet those with particular needs.

In their book *Succeeding with Difficult Students*, L. and M. Canter find that teacher management styles fall into three categories: non-assertive, hostile and assertive.

The non-assertive teacher is described as passive in response to student behaviour and discipline. They do not clearly communicate their expectations and are inconsistent in following through positive and negative reinforcement.

The hostile teacher usually responds at the expense of the students, and although not always aggressive and authoritarian may be sarcastic and petty.

Assertive teachers clearly, confidently and consistently state their expectations and are prepared to back their words with actions. Most teachers are a mixture of all three at different times. ADHD children need assertive teaching as much as humanly possible.

To be an effective teacher in school today you need to combine supreme efforts with a degree of instinct and luck. Every day, as a teacher you are faced with having to make a mountain of decisions. You may not get every one right.

Teachers need to share problems with others. Often, teachers attempt to work completely independently and do not allow others to become involved in successes or problems. It seems that some teachers expect to be able to do their job without interference from the rest of the school, or fear that telling colleagues they are having problems with a difficult student will be seen as an admission of failure. The fact is, children you are having difficulty with are most likely a problem for other teachers too. It is important that these difficulties do not emerge only after a major incident to which you react.

Tunnel of frustration

Imagine you are sitting on a train that has stopped inside a tunnel. As you sit there in the gloom, without a word of explanation, your anxiety and frustration grow. Should the situation continue, irritation, anger, even fear are likely. As soon as the driver's voice explains the cause for the delay, giving a time frame for normal service to be resumed, your anxiety and frustration subside. Although you are still stuck in the tunnel an explanation has been given.

Many teachers work within a 'tunnel of frustration' with regard to specific children. Once they find a connection or open a line of communication the results can be extremely beneficial to all involved: teacher, student and school.

Beware stress

Teachers should identify their stress levels and stay within set boundaries. One way to keep track of your stress is to keep an individualised points record. Allow yourself 10 stress points on an average day, a total of 50 for the working week. Keeping within this framework is very important. If you do 'blow your top' on a Monday it may mean you have borrowed stress points from Tuesday. In order to keep within the 50-point limit you will need to have a day with below-average stress later on in the week. If you use another 13 or 14 points on Tuesday or Wednesday, by Friday you will be running on empty. The net result of this will be illness or at very least early burnout.

Remember the following to avoid early teacher burnout:

① Eat well and get enough sleep.
② Exercise regularly.
③ Arrive at school early. Allow yourself some quiet time before the day begins.
④ Stay after school to unwind. Socialise, tie up loose ends, and prepare for the next day.
⑤ Know and accept your strengths and weaknesses. Trade your strengths with colleagues.
⑥ View mistakes as valuable learning experiences.
⑦ Find a colleague you can confide in.
⑧ Learn to say 'No'. Accept only the amount of responsibility that you can handle.
⑨ Associate with positive, enthusiastic people.
⑩ Never take anything negative from children, parents or colleagues personally. Teaching is a 'people job' and people will take a great deal from you if you allow them to get under your skin. If you take comments to heart and dwell on them, the chances are you will not last long.

Food For Thought

Bad days are a fact of life. After a particularly stressful day an ex-colleague of mine got the bus home from work and found himself snarled up in a traffic jam a mile away from his house. Cursing himself for not having driven to work, so that he avoided this particular route, he suddenly remembered that he had. The car was still sitting outside school. To make matters worse, his wife needed the car early the next morning. By now completely stressed out, my colleague got another bus back in to school to pick up the car, swearing all the way that he needed to find a new job.

Chapter 3
Social Factors

Socialisation issues

The fun part of going to school for many children is meeting other children. Therefore major problems will arise if children have difficulty in making and keeping friends. There are no rules for making friends – you choose or are chosen by those with whom you have something in common. Specific areas of interest – in sport, music, fashion, computer games and so on – bond students together. Common areas of interest can turn diverse individuals into groups.

A number of factors make integration into groups difficult for children with ADHD. A key problem is their inability to read the signals and cues of successful communication, cues that most of us understand subconsciously.

Often, children with ADHD are initially attractive to a group because of their unusual and amusing behaviour. This 'class clown' appeal soon wears thin, to be replaced by intolerance of the constant interruptions to group activity and conversation. This can lead to isolation.

Parents are often more concerned with how well their child is able to socialise than with academic achievement. They identify it, quite rightly, as a crucial way of developing self-esteem and happiness. They will often have experience of the problem. In many cases the child will have been excluded from invitations to the social gatherings of other children from the age of 2 on. Troubled relationships with siblings may compound the problem.

This section identifies specific socialisation issues and offers advice.

Danger areas

Children with ADHD are often out of step with the chronological age of their development. They may be best able to communicate with younger or older students. It is often hard for parents to understand why their child, who may be very articulate and at ease in the presence of adults, has problems socialising at school. In contrast, the adolescent student with ADHD is often the best student helper in the primary classroom.

Specific behaviour difficulties that emerge in class may be caused by events during the lesson, on the way in to school, during break time or that happened on the previous day.

Students are very territorial about where they sit in the classroom and about their storage areas. A student's own space within an otherwise very public school arena is highly treasured. It can be compared to their bedroom at home, where so often the rule is 'keep out'. One child sitting in another child's seat can be a major cause of confrontation, often involving an inattentive child with ADHD. The displaced child, usually quiet and mostly compliant, may become extremely agitated when denied their own seat, resulting in uncharacteristically aggressive behaviour. Calming the situation can take some time. The simple solution to this is to have a seating plan in all classrooms and keep to it.

Storage areas also need to be managed carefully. Ensure staff or older trusted students supervise locker areas, and that inspections are held only when absolutely necessary. Insulting other students' parents and name-calling will almost always guarantee a major confrontation and should be strongly discouraged.

Relationships between children are complex and difficult for adults to understand. Children themselves have a clearer understanding but even they have difficulty in fully explaining the specifics of why relationships fail or succeed. Children can be friends or enemies within minutes. They may be at each other's throats in school but spend time together at the weekend and share family trips. The situation seems to be in the lap of the gods.

These rapid and profound inconsistencies cause problems for parents. Delighted that their child has made a friend, parents will invite other children over to the house for a meal or for the weekend. The benefits of this need to be very carefully weighed against the costs. Careful planning and supervision are paramount for the friendship and your relationship with both children to continue. Return visits may also be perilous unless the other family understands the nature of the ADHD learning style. The same goes for parties and taking friends of your child on holiday.

While all children need supportive relationships, adolescents with ADHD are especially in need of guidance from caring adults, particularly when faced with academic and social adjustment problems. Often the successful student will say, 'I had someone who cared' or 'Someone believed in me.'

Supportive relationships are the cornerstone of academic success, and are at least as important as specific educational strategies. Strong emotional bonds between adults and children provide the safety zone in which failure and fears can be explored. This is where to plan how to react to problem situations, where motivation can be nurtured and encouragement given.

Socialisation is possibly the most difficult school subject. While there are no standard methods of preparation for successful course completion, some key pointers are listed below.

For parents

① Discourage all trade and money transactions between your child and their friends and siblings.

② Never invite more than three friends over to the house at one time, no matter how positive you may feel about your child.

③ If inviting friends of different sexes, make sure there is an equal number of boys and girls.

④ Despite the pressures on you and your child to bond with other pupils, be extremely careful about taking your child's friend on holiday with you. Unless you have had a great deal of contact with the friend and their family, factors may emerge that will cause problems and destroy the friendship altogether.

⑤ Set rules on when and how late your child is allowed out and stick to them. Do not be swayed by the child and, as a general rule, try to keep Sunday to Thursday evenings clear of distraction unless an organised, structured and properly supervised activity is available.

For teachers

① Keep to two in a group when teaching science and for any class group project work.

② Do not let children themselves pick teams during sports, quizzes and so on.

③ Supervise all unstructured periods – break and lunchtime – using your best personnel to monitor and possibly direct positive socialisation.

④ Do not attempt to force friendships between individual children. They will happen, or not, of their own accord. Sometimes children with ADHD will remain loners, no matter what.

⑤ Children staring or pulling faces at others are bound to cause trouble. Although this will happen occasionally, if a child is a regular offender it needs to be stopped.

⑥ Develop a proactive personal, social and health education (PSHE) programme in order to discuss the issues of bullying, peer pressure, smoking, drug use and sex education.

'The way I see it, if you want the rainbow, you gotta put up with the rain.'
Dolly Parton

For both parents and teachers

Discourage children from telling tales about each other. Students resent those who do not understand the code of silence that exists amongst children.

Lying and stealing

Though certainly not all children will be involved in stealing, being 'economical with the truth' is very common. Those with ADHD are poor liars as they can't remember sequences of events and are inconsistent. Crimes are not premeditated but impulsive. Risk-taking is a common characteristic; children will both commit the crime and lie later as a result.

The main reasons why children with ADHD do this are as follows:

① Forgetting the sequence of events.
② Protection.
③ To avoid punishment.
④ Boredom.

Forgetting the sequence of events

Due to short-term memory problems, some children genuinely cannot believe they did what they are accused of. They may construct highly imaginative versions of events. This does not mean that they should be excused the consequence of their actions. Whatever punishment assignment is set should reflect their learning style.

Protection

Having received much negative reinforcement during their lives, some students will say or do anything to protect their battered self-esteem. Alternatively, they may make things up in order to impress you.

To avoid punishment

This is the most obvious and widely experienced reason.

Boredom

Simple boredom may lead to all sorts of stories being told to avoid task completion or coming to class. Think positively and consider whether the boredom is well founded or not.

When trying to sort all this out the first rule is to avoid asking 'Did you do it?' when you know they did. Enforce the consequences quickly and firmly, without emotion. Confessions are difficult to get. It is far better to collate the evidence and present children with the facts. In lots of cases, evidence may be hard to find. In that case, as long as the crime is not too heinous, it is often best to drop the issue and move on.

Children with ADHD may be more prone to stealing than other children owing to their poor impulse control, indifference about consequences and low self-esteem. Similar strategies should be used to those for lying. Collate the evidence and avoid emotional verbal confrontations. Rules and penalties must be reinforced but the best strategy is blanket supervision at all times, and keeping valuables safe.

Additional socialisation problems arise through buying and selling items at school – this should be banned on school premises – and peer pressure to try new things like smoking, drugs and sex. These are complex issues that need to be dealt with sensitively as they arise.

Boys and girls

The differences between teaching girls and boys are obvious to all those who work with both, though often they are not highlighted by those who write about child behaviour. Girls still do better than boys in most national academic examinations. There are also different performance levels for specific subjects. It is not surprising that behaviour also differs widely. Girls react very differently from boys owing to the way in which they understand rules and the way in which they interpret their relationship with those who enforce them. This is particularly noticeable when dealing with boy and girl students with ADHD.

The number of HIT boys exceeds the number of HIT girls by approximately 4:1. The PIT ratio is more like 1:1. Many PIT girls go undiagnosed and are in danger of failing in our schools as a consequence. All girls and boys react differently to discipline and these differences are magnified for students with ADHD. Boys may be more physical and girls more verbal, in responses both to staff and other pupils. Girls often appear to be superior in verbal skills while the boys' lack of verbal skills may result in frustration expressed as explosive verbal or physical reaction when under pressure.

Case Study

These differences have been well illustrated for me through use of my favourite mechanical classroom assistant: a one-minute sand timer.

If a child has been misbehaving and needs to leave the classroom to calm down, place an upturned one-minute sand timer on the child's desk with the understanding that the student leaves by the time the sand runs out. This allows the student to save face in front of friends, whilst creating a controlled period of time for them to digest the consequences of not obeying the instruction.

In my experience, boys will allow the sand to run out before, with calmness but defiance, standing up slowly and loudly to leave.

Girls do not allow the sand to run out but will exclaim loudly, 'I'm not doing this.' They will get up dramatically, scraping their chair across the floor, tossing back their hair and storming outside, banging the door behind them.

The net result in both cases is that the students do as you request.

Social groups

Children form highly complex groups whose leaders and key players can influence the quality of school life to a massive degree. Time spent discussing and developing strategies to encourage or discourage specific group dynamics is worth at least one staff meeting every two weeks.

Changing a class structure because of an unstable group element can benefit both staff and other pupils. This element of the 'hidden curriculum' within student groups needs more attention than is usually provided if students with ADHD are to have any chance of success.

The point at which students are beginning to form relationships with members of the opposite sex also needs careful handling.

Case Study

Sandy and Michael were 17-year-olds. Both had poor academic histories at previous schools that meant completing their courses when they arrived at our school would be a major achievement. Michael was making progress but had a fragile relationship with his parents and with the staff. The arrival of an initially focused Sandy seemed to provide him with much needed stability and the two became friends immediately. This, unfortunately, became a hindrance as the association quickly became romantic and the effect spilled over into the classroom.

We tried to diffuse what became an awkward situation of PSA (public show of affection) but failed. One day, I found both of them out of their classroom during a lesson.

The teacher told me they had independently asked to go to the toilet. I was exasperated and said quietly, 'When Tweedledee and Tweedledum return to class, send them to me.' Unfortunately, I was not quiet enough. When the students returned, another student told Michael, 'When you were out Mr O'Regan said you were dumb.' Michael exploded and set off for my office. I had fuelled the situation and had to work hard to extinguish it.

Bullying

Poem 1

Walking down a corridor
Getting loathsome looks
Makes me feel the size of a pea
Makes me want to run and flee.

Anger rejection fear and pain
Nothing to learn and nothing to gain
All the teachers speak a lie
Makes me want to curl and die.

Why oh why am I me
All my pain no one can see
If only things had been different
looking ahead I hope they will!!!

Student aged 9

Poem 2

The forecast of this sunny day
Is turbulent weather, no chance to play?
Here it comes, not bright or clear
All it brings is fright and fear
Lightning, thunder, rains just pour!
It's not done this since '84
I've not seen a storm like this
To some this is complete bliss
Almost all rivers burst their banks
No one here has any rank
Sand bags thrown here and there
Water coming everywhere
The clouds brighten; up go the cheers
Now there are no frightened tears.

Student aged 14

Case Study

All schools have problems with bullying but children with ADHD are extremely vulnerable. The following example gives some perspective on the problem.

> Kieran had been very unhappy at his previous school. All the teachers thought he did not try hard in their classes although he was a very bright and self-motivated child. When I asked him why this was, he told me that he had made a choice for his survival. Other children had threatened that if he got good marks they would beat him up. They had done so on one occasion. If he didn't try to be a 'teacher's pet' he might be able to join their group.
>
> Kieran's main motivations at this point were fear of rejection from the pack and fear of physical assault. His teachers, he reasoned, could shout at him but couldn't touch him. The choice was clear.

According to statistics from the Department for Education and Skills (DfES) one-third of all girls and a quarter of all boys are afraid to got to school, at some point, because of bullying.

Bullying takes many forms. Generally, bullying amongst girls is more verbal and psychological, while boys adopt a more physical approach. The effects of both are extremely distressing for the victim, whose confidence and self-esteem play a crucial part in coping with the problem.

Alan Train, in his excellent book *The Bullying Problem* (1995), identifies two distinct groups of victims of bullies, which he calls 'passive' and 'provocative'. As he shows in his book, the characteristics of PIT ADHD students and passive victims, and those of HIT ADHD students and provocative victims, seem to have some similarities.

Passive victims are often 'spacey', insular and not part of a pack. They are prone to teasing from other students. Conversely, the provocative student who always blurts things out, or who is annoying because they are unable to read the signals of the group, will eventually irritate other children.

'Success is a science; if you have the conditions you get the result' Oscar Wilde

It is likely that the typical ADHD child will be a provocative victim. Most of the published research on bullying agrees that the way to proceed is to deal with both victim and bully in equal measure. As a long-term solution this is definitely the answer. However, in the short term the teacher needs to consider group dynamics as well as individuals. Below is a list of strategies that a class teacher or mentor could usefully teach the potential bullied student:

① How to stop and think before acting.
② How to identify problems and state how they feel.
③ How to set personal goals.
④ How to think of alternative solutions to conflict situations.
⑤ How to recognise pitfalls ahead of time.
⑥ How to develop a plan to avoid getting into hassles.

'Communication is the problem to the answer. Agree to disagree then disagree some more'.
The Things we do for Love,
Kevin Godley and Lol Creme

Food For Thought

Lucy was a hypoactive student with ADHD. She was drafted into the football team from the school for children with specific learning difficulties, to play against the local school. Her position was midfield but as far as she was concerned she was personally responsible for a zone of 5 square metres in the middle of the pitch, from which she never ventured. Lucy didn't look much of a threat. She appeared uninterested until shaken from her trance by someone yelling 'Lucy, ball!'

At this, Lucy hurtled in the direction of the ball but mostly clattered into the opposition. Afterwards she returned, trance-like, to her hypoactive state. Needless to say, with such a destructive weapon the game was largely decided by the reluctance of the local school to confront such forces of nature.

Break time, lunchtime and sports

Any change in the structure or routine of the standard school day needs to be carefully planned for the child with ADHD. Badly planned changes will undermine school systems and create a new set of potentially problematic variables.

Children facing a changed schedule often over-react in the most exaggerated fashion. Fire-alarm practice, examinations, the annual school photograph day, prize-giving day, sports day, talent shows and school field trips can be disastrous unless meticulously planned. My least favourite school term is the summer term, in which many of these events take place.

For the same reason, careful consideration must be given to all non-classroom time such as breaks and lunchtime, and sports activities where socialisation problems can occur. Break and lunchtimes should be structured as much as possible. This may mean scheduling your most effective staff to supervise during these times. Having a selection of games like Othello, chess, Connect 4 and computer games is useful.

Letting hyperactive children run around for a mere 15 minutes in the playground will not burn off energy. In reality, children pumped up during break are extremely difficult to settle back in the classroom. Unsupervised playground games, like football and basketball, present many problems for children who may find themselves excluded and victimised.

Of course, not all children with ADHD are poor at sports. Sufficient interest in a specific sport can act as a focus for energies. One-to-one sports or individualised activities like ten-pin bowling, swimming, fishing and biking are recommended as maximum involvement is ensured. Team games need to be highly interactive.

Many children will have some gross motor co-ordination difficulties so activities should not include table tennis, lawn tennis, squash and golf, all of which require good hand-eye co-ordination skills. Martial arts like judo and karate are well worth considering. It appears that the discipline, structure and philosophy of the eastern self-defence sports relate well to the ADHD learning style.

 Any period of non-involvement during sports activities will result in mental drift and students looking for something else to do. Sports with prolonged inactivity, like fielding in cricket or softball, are to be avoided. Whether supervising on the sports field or on a school trip, precise instructions are needed to enable children to cope with all of the additional distractions of being outside the classroom. It is essential that they process the vital information. Keep it short and simple and make sure children have their eyes fixed on you. To make sure 'mental drifters' are listening, ask all children to hold their hands in the air while you are talking.

Field trips

It is a missed opportunity when children with ADHD are excluded from field trips. These events must be regarded not just as fun days out but as opportunities to train children to manage experiences that will help them to understand and develop socially.

Trips with activities that involve supporting instructors – like ski trips or activity holidays – are preferable. These structured vacations are better than trips that involve sightseeing or periods where lots of free time is available. Day trips to hands-on centres are preferable to those to museums or art galleries. Teachers should choose a trip because of the interests of the students, not because a discount is offered or the teacher is interested in going there.

The following nine-point list will be useful when planning trips.

① What is the purpose of the trip and how does it fit current educational goals?
② Where is the site located and what is the distance to and from school?
③ Which is the best mode of transport to get there?
④ On what days and dates and at what times is the site available?
⑤ How much time is needed for a visit and are there any special considerations?
⑥ What are the costs for pupils and adults?
⑦ What introduction is needed and what follow-up activities can be devised for students?
⑧ What is the food provision?
⑨ What other supplies or equipment are needed?

The home

The impact of the child with ADHD on the home environment has filled many a book and cannot be covered in great detail here. But here are a few suggestions on some aspects of home management:

① Put into perspective issues that may be annoying but not life threatening.
② Be proactive, not reactive.
③ Acquire the patience of a saint (and invest in a Golden Retriever).

Examples of situations that may be annoying but not overly important in the long run include the messy bedroom, musical preferences, poor grammar, not going on family outings, poor eating habits, dress sense, use of allowance, using other people's things without asking and not doing chores at regular times. React to the child you have and not the child that you would like them to be.
Parents almost invariably love their children, but it can be very hard to like them all the time. Patience, in these circumstances, is an absolute must.

Once in a while watch your child while they sleep. It is a powerful regenerating experience to see this person, who throughout the day behaves like a spinning top, finally at peace, still your loving and loved child.

A pet is a good idea, especially for older children. Dogs with calm

Food For Thought

1. Keep things in perspective. Consider the 'use of the phone' issue. If your child calls a friend they have been with all day, and the conversation appears meaningless and lasts for an age – relax! This is what all kids do. They are making contact with one another and learning about relationships. These connections are good for their self-esteem. If you are concerned about the phone bill then move to strategy 2.
2. Be proactive. Make a deal that the child pays for the charges over and above a certain amount.

temperaments offer unconditional love and do not judge the child in the way that peers, siblings and parents do. Of course, don't assume the child will look after the pet's needs without a proactive reward system in force.

Brothers and sisters

Sibling relationships are difficult for all concerned. The child with ADHD will be affected by the academic performance of his non-ADHD brothers and sisters. This can result in envy, resentment and poor self-esteem. For the siblings the situation can also be tough – they have to try to be patient with an unruly brother or sister who appears to dominate their parents' time so that parents often seem to have little energy for them. Parents may feel torn.

The home situation may be torrid for all concerned. As a result, although school may have its problems, for the child with ADHD compared with home it may well be a haven.

Case Studies

'It seemed as if World War Three had started when Kevin found out that his seventeenth birthday present was not going to be driving lessons. He told us in no uncertain terms, in between screaming and sobbing, that this was "just not fair" as his two older siblings had both been given driving lessons at the same age – which was true. Unfortunately Kevin is a different story. We can't really let him go to the local shop and back alone much less let him loose onto the roads behind the wheel of a car. It would not be safe for Kevin or the rest of East Croydon.'

'We know Simon feels we pick on him. He says we prefer his younger sister because she never gets in trouble and gets good marks in all her subjects. We really don't, of course, but it is difficult to treat the children in the same way when they behave so differently.'

Chapter 4
Other Organisations, Professionals and Parents

Assessment

Thorough assessment is necessary to determine whether a child has ADHD. Traumatic as labels are, it is often a relief to have an objective account to explain behaviours that appear odd.

Chris Green, in his book *Understanding ADHD*, identifies the four basic steps of diagnosis as follows:

① Looking for alarm signals.
② Excluding ADHD lookalikes.
③ Using objective pointers.
④ Taking a detailed history of the individual concerned.

A fifth step might usefully be added, which is that diagnosis is only as useful as the educational resources subsequently made available. A diagnosis that does not allow for practical applications in relation to conclusions will add to the frustration of the parents and their children. Specialist professionals are essential for the successful identification of ADHD. They need to advise and direct the provision of practical support mechanisms to teachers and parents.

Psychologists

Educational and clinical psychologists, consultant paediatricians and psychiatrists may all be involved in the assessment process. Only the last two in this list may prescribe medication if appropriate. Psychologists may only recommend its use.

Parents may act independently and seek the help of these professionals. But before seeking professionals' help, teachers must follow the guidelines of the 2001 Code of Practice for the Identification and Assessment of Special Educational Needs (SEN), some features of which are outlined below.

The old five-stage process for identifying SEN children, used since 1994, has been superceded by measures in the new Code of Practice. Identification of pupils with SEN now begins with School Action, which follows consultation between the teachers, parent and SENCo and leads to an Individual Education Plan (IEP) being devised. The pupil's work is monitored and parents are encouraged to work with the child at home. The IEP is reviewed at least twice a year. Parents must always be invited to these reviews. Teaching Assistants (TAs) may be involved at this stage. If the pupil fails to make progress the school will apply to the LEA to move onto School Action Plus. If the LEA decides this is appropriate, a visiting professional will offer advice to the school regarding the targets on the IEP and will usually monitor the pupil's progress. At this stage, various outside professionals may become involved.

'Only the person who has faith in himself is able to be faithful to others'
Erich Frohm

Once diagnosis has taken place, great care must be taken to ensure that expectations for the child are at the right level. For example, if no-one expects the child to concentrate, there will be a danger of no-one trying to get them to do so. It is all too easy for diagnosis to create a handicap.

Parents going through an independent route should note that a credible diagnosis of ADHD is not possible after one 30-minute or even 60-minute doctor's appointment with little background information. This does happen. Some parents have their child diagnosed after a short visit to a professional, primarily on the basis of the child's behaviour during the interview. They may even go straight to a medication option on this basis.

Central to any evaluation of behaviour is an analysis of the history of the child, including the age of onset of behaviour that causes concern, behaviour in a range of settings and the record of remedial treatment. Full details of how previous strategies fared must be studied. The observations of previous teachers and other adults familiar with the child should be taken into account.

It is strongly recommended that before any assessment takes place parents should approach relevant professionals and ask them to describe the procedures they intend to use.

A medical evaluation must always start any assessment process. This is necessary to make sure that no lookalike conditions are causing the symptoms. Tests should be made for allergies and other medical conditions. Eyesight and hearing must be checked.

Case Study

I interviewed Kirsty some years ago. She had been diagnosed as ADHD by a local educational psychologist. Kirsty had a poor record of behaviour problems owing to her persistent inattention and lack of concentration. We advised that she join our summer school programme. Very quickly I began to feel that Kirsty did not have ADHD and suggested that she be taken for medical assessment. As it turned out, Kirsty had only 55 per cent hearing in her left ear and 35 per cent in her right. The doctor believed her hearing had been deteriorating for the past four years.

Kirsty wasn't concentrating in class because she couldn't hear what was going on. She didn't know she had less-than-perfect hearing.

Following a medical evaluation the gathering of information from various sources should begin. Sources should include the following:
① The parents, by interview and checklists.
② Discussions with the child.

③ Previous school and teacher reports. This should involve making a call to the previous school and speaking to the head or class teacher personally.

It has been my experience that parents may not show some reports, feeling they would prefer the assessor did not read them. This is a mistake. Schools should be acting in the best interests of the child, so revealing the full history is the best policy.

Once this has happened, psychometric testing should take place to assess IQ and visual, auditory and visual motor (writing) skills, and current achievement. This will reveal whether the child has a specific learning difficulty, like dyslexia, that may be the main problem. This may be present alongside ADHD. Computerised testing should also take place to access impulsivity, attention to detail and vigilance. Coupled with a complete background history generated by checklists, interviews and past reports, these contribute to a comprehensive analysis.

Educational psychologists' reports will suggest a diagnosis and make recommendations in terms of educational and socialisation provision. In addition, they may suggest specialist counselling and medication. Psychologists are in a difficult position and are often not popular with the children they test. Students are often reluctant to do 'silly exercises'. Teachers too may have uneasy relationships with psychologists.

Counsellors

Counsellors may play a vital role in helping children come to terms with their learning styles and with the general trials and tribulations of life. They may also help by linking behaviour plans and expectations between school and home. Whilst it is essential for teachers and parents to work together, it is important that teachers do not become involved in home life. The counsellor has an important role to play here.

Specialist family counselling also has its place in the equation. Many excellent programmes exist to help parents come to terms with problems in their relationship with their child and with other members of the family. Home management techniques can be taught through role-play and to some extent through group therapy. Overall, the success of these programmes depends largely on the quality of the counsellor.

Anger is one of the core features of children with ADHD. Anger may be directed at parents, siblings, teachers and peers. Whether or not this anger is justified is immaterial. It is always very real to the individual expressing it. Children often develop their own methods to deal with anger.

Case Studies

> Adam told his counsellor that he kept his anger in a 'special place'. This was a place as far away as possible from his head, so that he could control it. When pressed to find out where this was, he said, 'I keep all of my anger in my feet.' He explained, 'It has to go a long way to get out my mouth from there.'
>
> Aktir, when trying to justify why his impulsivity had got the better of him, causing him to lash out again, said in tears, 'It's just that the bad side of my body is stronger than the good side of my body.'

BEFORE   AFTER

Parental break-up – a common feature of the families of children with ADHD – change of school or teachers, bereavement, problems with peers inside and outside school, are all issues that may result in fear, frustration and angry outbursts.

The role of the counsellor may be a lonely one. Much of the information with which they are entrusted is confidential, and it takes a very special person to do the job well. However, it is a vital component in the overall multi-management process. Cutting corners here can undo a lot of the good work done elsewhere.

Medication

For many children with ADHD medication is an important part of the treatment. Medication should not be used to control behaviour but to improve the symptoms of ADHD. Research shows that children who take medication for the symptoms of ADHD attribute their successes to themselves and not to the medication.

A paediatrician may recommend medication after studying the findings of the observation processes outlined above. Medication should be considered only if educational programmes, behaviour modification and counselling strategies have been shown to have failed. It should follow the sequence outlined below:

① Diagnosis.
② Remediation.
③ Structured learning environment.
④ Counselling.
⑤ Observation.
⑥ Is medication necessary?
⑦ Establishment of base rate of medication.
⑧ Trial period.
⑨ Adjustment of dosage.
⑩ Do the benefits of medication outweigh the drawbacks?
⑪ Is medication still necessary?
⑫ Medication may be suspended for a period annually.

There should be a continuous process of assessment to record the use of medication. After the trial period at stage 8, any side-effects should be noted and adjustments made. A decision about whether or not significant positive changes in work completion, concentration and behaviour are evident determines whether medication should be continued. Medication should be suspended for a period every 12 months to measure whether the child has been able to adapt to the strategies that medication has made available.

Medication for ADHD is a highly contentious area guaranteed to divide those involved. It is a decision made for individual children by parents and a medical practitioner. Whatever personal feelings people may have about it, the decision should be regarded as a pragmatic option taken by those parties most responsible for the child. Although medicating students for academic benefit is frowned upon by many educationalists, over the years some students have benefited from the increased focus, attention and self-esteem medication can help to bring.

Research shows that neurotransmitters in the brain are responsible for relaying information necessary for certain behaviours, for example impulse control and concentration. Dysregulation in this complex chemical relay system appears to cause emotional and behavioural problems. Paul Cooper argues in *Therapeutic Care and Education*, 4, 1995, 'medication is employed not as a chemical cosh to sedate overactive or inattentive children but as a chemical facilitator that raises chronically low levels of activity in certain parts of the brain and so regulates the message-carrying process'. If ADHD is accepted as a neurobiochemical condition caused by lack of specific neurotransmitters, then a neurobiochemical solution may often be appropriate.

How the medication actually works is something of a mystery. One theory is that chemical stimulants like Ritalin, the most common of the drugs used for treatment of ADHD, speed up the metabolic uptake of glucose in the frontal region of the brain, facilitating greater impulse control and better levels of concentration.

The neurostimulants Methylphenidate (Ritalin) and Dexamphetaphine (Dexedrine) are the most commonly used drugs. Equasym® (a bioequivalent of Ritalin), Concerta, Adderall and Cylert are alternatives.

Not all children enjoy taking medication, even though it may be helping them academically, behaviourally and socially. Some students do not like to feel different and are aware of the emotional pressure of becoming more focused. They may be embarrassed about taking medication in front of their peers. Minorities of students suffer from a range of side-effects such as stomach upsets. This happens especially in the early stages of use.

Hundreds of studies on thousands of children have been conducted into the effects of psychostimulant medication. Relatively few long-term side-effects have been identified. According to the current state of research, most problems with medication are mild and short term. The most common side-effects are reduction in appetite and difficulty in sleeping. Less frequently, students experience a stimulant rebound with mood swings or an increase in activity when the medication is losing effect. There may be an initial slight slowing of growth and weight gain, but studies show that ultimate height and weight are rarely affected.

Case Studies

On the whole, children for whom medication is correctly prescribed are positive about its effect:

'When I'm on it [Ritalin], I work harder, and I'm nicer; but when I'm out of school [and not on Ritalin] I'm sometimes silly, or I act stupid, or do things that I wouldn't do when I'm on it.'

'When I'm taking Ritalin I'm calmer. I can study more and when I'm not, I really can't concentrate on anything.'

'I can concentrate better on Ritalin. I get on with my work more, and I don't talk so much.'

It is important to note that few long-term studies have been carried out. The use of medication calls for constant vigilance and there is a continued need for independent research.

The most serious potential side-effect is the unmasking of latent tics or involuntary motor movements such as eye blinking, shrugging and clearing of the throat. Psychostimulant medications will sometimes provoke a tic. Often, but not always, the tic will disappear when the medication is stopped. Tourette's syndrome is a chronic disorder that involves vocal and motor tics. Some experts estimate that 1 per cent of children with ADHD have Tourette's. It must be emphasised that the development of Tourette's is not directly linked to the use of the medication.

Other medication options include anti-depressants, often used when psychostimulants have proven ineffective, when conditions exist in tandem or when unacceptable side-effects have resulted from stimulants. Clonidine®, an anti-hypertensive medication, is sometimes used; its use is for intrusive and hyperactive behaviour rather than selective attention. Sometimes Clonidine® and a psychostimulant will be used in combination for children who have a range of symptoms.

For any child on medication the parents are in charge, not the doctors, psychologists or teachers. Although the decision about whether or not medication is prescribed rests with the physician, the parents may choose whether to follow the professional's advice or not.

'Never judge a day until the evening'
Anonymous

Statistics suggest that stimulant medication is effective in improving academic performance for about 75 per cent of students with hyperactive/impulsive (HIT) ADHD and about 60 per cent for students with inattentive (PIT) ADHD. Stimulant medication may not always be the answer to helping students with either direct or co-behaviour problems. Behaviour patterns like Oppositional Defiant Disorder (ODD) and Conduct Disorder (CD) are often associated with ADHD but also exist independently. Details of ODD and CD may be found in the Diagnostic criteria section on pages 60 and 61.

Alternative treatments

Alternative treatments include reducing overactivity through the adaptation of diet; use of megavitamins/mineral supplements or anti-motion-sickness medication; treatment of candida albicans; EEG biofeedback; applied kinesiology; optometric vision training and many more. There are as many opponents as there are proponents for these treatments. More research is needed into their usefulness. Parents should make a thorough investigation for themselves before using any of the treatments. Below is a very short survey of some of the more common alternative treatments used.

Dietary adaptation

For over 25 years Benjamin Feingold and others have argued that artificial food flavourings and colourings are responsible for a broad range of children's learning, behaviour and attention problems. Most of the recent research suggests that only a small group of children are affected. However, pumping extra sugar in the form of sweets and carbonated drinks into already hyperactive individuals is not going to improve attention to detail. Generally, children need a healthy and controlled diet. If modifying diet dramatically helps your child, continue to do that.

Megavitamins/mineral supplements

Because vitamins are natural substances synonymous with health, this approach has clear appeal. Vitamin deficiency can cause an array of problems, so it is an attractive idea that it may also cause learning and attention difficulties. However, three major studies have showed no evidence of vitamin supplements having any success in treating ADHD.

Anti-motion-sickness medication

Advocates of this theory believe that ADHD is caused by problems in the inner ear, and that there is a correlation between co-ordination and balance and thus attention. Research studies have made no conclusive findings. However, much research does suggest that attention and impulse control are regulated through frontal systems in the brain.

Candida albicans

This is a yeast occurring naturally in the body that many believe produces toxins that weaken the immune system and make the body susceptible to illnesses, and to ADHD and other psychiatric disorders. Treatment is designed to stop the growth of candida. It involves using anti-fungal medicine to kill yeasts without harming friendly bacteria, and a low sugar diet to discourage yeast growth. Although the evidence points to candida being responsible for some physical conditions, there is little evidence that treatment can be effective against ADHD.

'He has half the deed done who has made a beginning'
Horace

EEG biofeedback

Proponents of this method believe that children can be trained to increase the brain-wave activity associated with sustained attention and to decrease that associated with day-dreaming and distraction. They claim the result is improved attention and reduction in hyperactivity and impulsivity. The technique involves measuring levels of electrical activity in various parts of the brain. Children are trained to alter these using rewards. Evidence is patchy but has shown positive results. Treatment is expensive.

Cranial Osteopathy

This argues that learning difficulties arise from the misalignment of two specific bones in the skull. This creates pressure on the brain, leading to malfunctions. Treatment consists of restoring the cranial bones through manipulation. There is no evidence of its effectiveness.

Optometric vision training

Behavioural optometrists argue that reading disorders are due to visual problems, such as faulty eye movements and eyes being sensitive to certain visual frequencies. Treatment varies but options include eye exercises and coloured lenses. The evidence for its effectiveness is patchy. Most believe that the majority of reading disorders are caused by deficiencies in the storage and retrieval of linguistic material. A number of studies suggest optometric programmes are ineffective.

As with any other 'cure' for ADHD, it is essential to research these methods carefully before using any of them.

Speech and language therapists, occupational therapists

Dyslexia is often associated with ADHD. It is thought that problems in the storage (memory) and processing of linguistic information are factors in dyslexia. Therefore, speech and language therapists have a crucial role. They can help with verbal communication skills and so greatly influence a child's socialisation process.

Speech and language therapists can provide strategies that may be applied in the classroom. The personality of the therapist and the relationship they build with school and parents are all important. Teaching students with ADHD is a qualitative and multi-professional undertaking. Professionals who work in isolation will not be effective. Some speech and language therapists have made a major contribution to the treatment of learning difficulties in the UK. Bevé Hornsby and Helen Arkell, household names within the special needs teaching world, started their careers as speech therapists.

Occupational therapy covers a large area, involving visual, hearing and motor handicaps, learning disabilities, specific learning difficulties and children with cultural and emotional difficulties. For children with ADHD help with the fine visual and motor skills needed for handwriting is provided, along with help in visual perception, neurological and postural control, and the planning and organisation of tasks. Some students may never write well owing to their learning style. Teaching typing early on is one useful option for these. A combination of medication and intensive visual motor direction is often the most effective method to improve handwriting in practice. As with speech and language therapists, the personality of the occupational therapist and their working relationship with the school and parents are all important.

Parents

Like students and teachers, parents come in all shapes and sizes. Some are constantly tormented by their child and can barely cope. Some fight their child's corner with a will, sometimes blinding themselves to a clear understanding through their loyalty. Some simply refuse to accept that their child has a problem. But no matter what type they are, parents almost all act out of their perception of their child's best interests.

It is most often mothers who bear the brunt of the problem and most forcefully seek a solution. At my school, in four out of five admission interviews with new families, the mother attends alone. Where at all possible, fathers should be involved as well.

Case Study

'I'm at the end of my rope with Liam ... I've told him I can deal with anything other than lying and after all the times I've told him this, he still does it ... even when you present him with the facts he will still not admit it. Worse still it's always someone else's fault ... I don't know why he does it. I really feel like giving up'.

Some research suggests that children with ADHD behave better with their fathers. This can cause conflict between parents. The father blames the mother for not keeping the child under control while the mother feels guilty and helpless. Fathers, despite their potential influence, may react to ADHD by not going home until the child is asleep or by siding with the child against the mother. Mothers socialise with other mothers who are raising their families with apparent ease. This can deepen maternal self-doubt, anxiety and depression. In turn, these feelings may be communicated to the child so that the situation deteriorates further. Some parents become socially isolated, demoralised and tyrannised by their offspring. In extreme cases the family will break up.

Thomas Phelan's book *1–2–3 Magic: Effective Discipline for Children 2–12* (1996) argues that most parents, not just those of children with ADHD, think of their kids 'as little adults'. They are not. Children lack the ability to reason and live in a world dominated by their own needs and desires. If you add in the hyperactivity, impulsivity and argumentative nature of the child with ADHD, you have an explosive cocktail. Parents of all children need to educate their children in the ways to behave. What is needed is a 'benign dictatorship', not a democracy. The philosophy needs to be proactive, not reactive.

Case Studies

'Stopped being invited to the other children's parties from the age of 3 – too disruptive.'

'Nobody wants to come to the house to play with him.'

'I know they all think I am a bad mother.'

Case Studies

'He's easily lead but always gets the blame.'

'I can never take him to the shops.'

These are just some of the comments made by harassed mothers about raising the child with ADHD. One mother said, 'Every time I hear or see a fire engine, I instinctively wonder if my child is responsible.'

'Children need love most when they deserve it least'
Anonymous

Case Study

One issue that may be a major factor in the life of the child with ADHD is that one or other of the parents may also exhibit many of the signs of hyperactivity, impulsivity and inattention seen in their child. It is not uncommon during the admissions interview, after the parents have arrived late and without the correct paperwork, to observe the father of the child rocking back on his chair, staring at the ceiling whilst fiddling with the hanging cord of the venetian blind. When you meet the child, you are looking at the younger version. I think the appropriate expression is that the acorn does not fall too far from the tree.

One mother said, 'I'm sure that Donny gets it from his dad. My husband Bill is a really wonderful guy and the kids love him to bits but it's like having another child in the house. He forgets everything I ask him to do, whether it's to pick up the milk or, on the extremely rare occasions that I ask him, getting the kids home from school. Last week my daughter called me from the school car park because he'd forgotten to pick her up again. He is worse than useless with money. I have to pay all the bills or we'd be broke.'

As the literature has shown ADHD to be more common in boys, it is of course more likely to be prominent in fathers than in mothers. This is probably one of the reasons why fathers appear to be absent from any school function or parent-teacher meeting. Past experience of the educational environment does not exactly have them rushing back into the buildings.

Whenever this kind of information comes to light, the poor dad, who is doing the right thing by attending the admissions interview, is likely to find his arm being punched by his partner. After this may come a statement to the effect of 'See, after all we've been through, it is all your fault.' The teacher's line should always be that this a shared situation and both parents are in it together.

In the last few years we have noticed an increase in the number of single fathers bringing up teenage ADHD daughters. The relationships have been interesting to observe.

Some fathers can become extremely frustrated with their ADHD sons and daughters. They will certainly let you know this during any meeting at the school. The mother who, in my experience, on average spends approximately 400 per cent more time with the particular child, looks on patiently while the father rants on about the evils of falling standards and the Internet.

With Sarah and her father, it was war from beginning to end as both of them were highly impulsive and explosive. Somehow Sarah made it through to the end of the third term. There were tears of joy and relief that both of them had made it – not from them, but from the staff of the school.

Teachers need to build strong relationships with the child. Part of this process may include helping parents to cope at home. Parents need someone at school who is not going to judge them for their child's behaviour.

Case Study

For Mr Bailey and his 10-year old son, Freddie, the issue was that both of them were highly charged individuals who would not back down in the course of an argument. Each wanted the final word. When Freddy got it that would send his father into a frenzy, as he felt he should have this right, being the 'head of the family'.

I suggested to the father that he pay Freddy 50p to give him, the father, the right to the last word. (Money, if used carefully, can be an effective home management tool.) Two weeks later the father called me to say thank you. Things at home were calmer and he and Freddy were getting along fine. He then said that the sight of Freddy biting his lip in order to get the 50p was worth every penny and he would have paid up to £5 for this outcome.

I told him not to tell Freddy.

Teachers should let the parents know when both negative and positive things happen at school. Parents become wary and defensive when teachers always call with bad news. If an occasional call is made about good behaviour or an assignment well done, a much more productive relationship is possible. A well-established relationship enables the parent and teacher to work together even when a major problem arises. Without strong links, progress for the student will be slow. Also, the student will exploit any weakness in the parent–school relationship. Any opportunity to play off school against home will be seized.

There are lots of books, some including specialised kits, on how to manage the child with ADHD at home. One of the best I have read is Thomas Phelan's *1–2–3 Magic*. It offers a highly effective non-verbal approach for the management of inappropriate behaviour, both in the home and the classroom. ADHD support groups also offer much needed support and advice. (A list of these can be found in the Support groups section on page 62.)

Here are a few ideas for helping to build successful relationships between schools and parents:

Parents

Ask yourself what really matters. Is it more important for the child to arrive at school calm and cheerful or tidy their room before leaving the house?

Teachers

Be prepared to admit to being in the wrong and willing to change your strategy if it is not working. Keep an open mind.

Teachers and parents

① Give the child frequent and consistent feedback and impress on them the positive and negative consequences of their behaviour.

② Reward rather than punish. Rewards are deserved and legitimate positive consequences.

③ Criticise the behaviour, not the child. Practise forgiveness.

④ Take care of yourself. Only if you do this will you be in any position to activate any of the above.

⑤ Cherish a sense of humour. Keep things in perspective.

Current issues

It is still the case that many professionals and much of the public view the term ADHD with mistrust. Some of the objections were outlined by P. Cooper and T. Shea in their article ADHD from the Inside: An Empirical Study of Young People's Perception of ADHD, *Research Practice and Opinion* (1999). They were as follows:

① It individualises behavioural problems and so underplays the importance of the educational and broader social environment in causing and remedying these problems.

② The use of medication in the treatment of ADHD serves a social control function by keeping potentially disruptive and troublesome individuals docile.

③ It allows both bearers of the label and their carers to abdicate from their responsibility to take charge of the problems associated with ADHD by allowing them to blame the condition on causes that are outside their sphere of influence.

Studies done to look at the origins of behaviour problems that are most prevalent and disruptive in childhood are consistent with the diagnostic criteria of ADHD outlined in Chapter 1. The largest British survey of teachers' views on discipline in schools, carried out by Gray and Sime for the Department of Education and Science in 1989, listed behaviours leading to disruption to be as follows:

① Talking out of turn and distracting others.

② Calculated idleness and work avoidance.

③ Hindering other pupils.

④ Making unnecessary noise.

⑤ Persistently infringing school rules.

⑥ Getting out of seat without permission.

⑦ Verbal abuse to other pupils.

⑧ Cheeky or impertinent remarks or responses.

Food For Thought

With Ryan you could tell from his body language what sort of a day we were in for. Shoulders slumped, scowl on the face – it was going to be hard to teach him today. After a painful series of incidents and a lot of digging we traced his bad moods back to confrontations with his sister in the morning before he left for school. From then on, his mother would call the school before he arrived if there had been an incident. This enabled us to act, putting Ryan into a 'time out' situation where he could wind down for the first period of the day.

'The way to love anything is to realise that it might be lost'
G.K. Chesterton

'Few of us have the greatness to truly blend history itself. But if each one of us selects one small part of the country and works to change one set of circumstances ... the collective efforts of all of us will write the history of his generation'
Robert F. Kennedy

Although this does not mean that all behaviours of this type signal ADHD, it does indicate that the types of behaviours associated with ADHD are of critical concern to teachers as they signify the disruption of the educational process. In *ADHD: A Practical Guide for Teachers* (1996), P. Cooper and K. Ideus argue that the reception of ADHD in the UK by British educationalists is the historical rejection of the medical profession by education. Today, educationalists believe that if you get the curriculum right and class sizes down you will solve all problems. In my view, the sensible alternative is to look for the opportunity for teachers to incorporate a medical perspective into the existing framework and, in doing so, develop effective interdisciplinary collaboration with medical practitioners and psychologists.

The publication of guidance on the use of Ritalin and Equasym® by the National Institute for Clinical Excellence (NICE) in October 2000 was a helpful contribution. The referral of this issue for expert and independent appraisal was one of a range of initiatives taken by the DfES aimed at improving the recognition and understanding of attention deficit disorders and ensuring that appropriate treatment is more widely available. In summary, NICE concluded that Ritalin should be used as part of a comprehensive treatment programme for children with a diagnosis of severe ADHD. In addition the following was stated:

① The drug should be discontinued if improvement of symptoms is not observed after appropriate dose adjustment over one month.
② Children on Ritalin therapy should receive regular monitoring.
③ Diagnosis should be based on comprehensive assessment by a specialist.
④ Treatment should be initiated by specialists, but GPs may be involved in continuing to prescribe and monitor under shared-care arrangements.

Another important development has been the setting up of the ADHD National Alliance. The alliance was created following the hard work of a number of parent-support and information groups, primarily the Contact a Family group. It has received an initial three-year grant from the Department of Health. The main function of the alliance is to raise awareness and develop information, support and provision for ADHD sufferers.

There is still much to do. The government's current Code of Practice for Special Educational Needs (2001) makes no mention of ADHD, although there is direct mention of dyslexia, emotional and behavioural difficulties and speech and language problems.

Inclusion

The current policy of inclusion into mainstream schooling of children with special educational needs, although laudable in theory, will be very difficult to achieve in practice for children with ADHD. There are two main reasons for this:

① The management of ADHD is a qualitative process that requires everyone, from the playground supervisor to the head of the French department, to be in on the game plan. Anything from 8 to 50 adults (depending on the size of the school) will need knowledge, understanding and acceptance of ADHD and the child involved. Though the new SEN Code of Practice promotes this, it is difficult to see this working even in small, traditional schools. The variables and communication systems involved are too great.

② Children with traditional learning styles will not have been included in planning how to deal with what looks like a perfectly normal-looking child who is always interrupting them, getting on their nerves and disrupting their lessons.

Of course, all things are possible. With proper training of staff and proactive PSHE programmes obstacles can be overcome. Simply saying inclusion has to work is not enough. Proper support needs to be made available. Inclusion has to be regarded as a process, not a policy. Funds must be made available for special educational provision so that children with ADHD are not sacrificed on the altar of inclusion.

Training issues must be urgently addressed. Information, seminars and dedicated teacher-training programmes for every newly qualified teacher, as well as for teachers already in post in mainstream schools, are all essential.

The picture is not bleak. Many students with ADHD have a positive experience during their school years, despite the odds, and become successful and highly motivated adults. I shall leave you with an account of one.

Case Study

A recent visitor to my school arrived looking splendid in the full captain's uniform of Virgin Airlines. His ex-teacher did not recognise him at first, until the visitor spoke. The teacher's blood chilled. The distinctive voice was unmistakably that of a former student whose school career, eight years previously, had left the teacher licking his wounds. Now he was an airline captain–the product of the student's obsessive love of planes and a Virgin Airlines work-experience placement.

As the former student left the school, despite his change in personality and success, the teacher vowed that if he were ever on a plane and the former student's voice came over the intercom, the teacher would jump out of the plane, parachute or not. He could forgive–but never forget!

How to teach and manage children with ADHD   51

Chapter 5
Support Materials

In this chapter is material to help with teaching students with ADHD.
A number of checklists and forms and some supplementary information are
supplied: Teaching resources (pages 51 to 59), Diagnostic criteria for other
disorders (pages 60 and 61) and Support groups (pages 62 and 63).

Situation Analysis Response

Below is a useful way to structure your analysis of and response to a child's
behaviour.

Familiar patterns seen

....
....
....
....
....
....
....

What is the best way to solve this problem? What are the key issues? What
should my strategies be?

How should I order my approach?

a)

b)

c)

d)

e)

f)

Are there any back-up strategies I should keep in reserve?

....
....
....
....
....

© How to teach and manage children with ADHD   LDA

The ideal teacher

The ideal teacher (and parent) for a child with ADHD

- Thoroughly knowledgeable about ADHD and accepts legitimacy of the disorder.
- Tough as nails about rules but always calm and positive.
- Ingenious about modifying teaching strategies and materials in order to match child's learning style.
- Creates assignments that call for as much activity on child's part as possible.
- Deals with homework in a pragmatic way.
- Tailors academic material to suit child's abilities and skills.
- Mixes high- and low-interest tasks in tune with child's learning style.
- Knows when to back off when student's level of frustration begins to peak.
- Knows when to back off when teacher's (or parent's) level of frustration begins to peak.
- Speaks clearly in brief, understandable sentences.
- Looks the child straight in the eye when communicating.
- Runs an absolutely predictable and organised classroom.
- Controls the classroom without being controlling.
- Provides immediate and consistent feedback regarding behaviour.
- Develops a private signal system with child to gently notify him/her when he/she is off task or acting inappropriately.
- Maintains close proximity without being intrusive.
- Ignores minor disruptions. Knows when to take a stand and when not.

Computers

How is the computer beneficial?

- ADHD child responds to the individualised setting.
- Attention is focused on the screen.
- Multi-sensory experience.
- Non-threatening: can retry problems, constant feedback and reinforcement.
- Impersonal: computer doesn't yell or have favourites.
- Variety of presentation: attend better to novel stimuli.
- Student can control pace.
- Flexible: programmed to do many things.
- Rapid assessment.
- Game-like approach: challenging.

Caution

Software needs to be carefully chosen.
Guard against frustrations arising from technical problems.
Teach keyboard skills to avoid frustration.
Computers are not a substitute for teaching.

Behaviour

Supervision and discipline

- Remain calm, don't debate or argue with student.
- Have pre-established consequences for misbehaviour.
- Administer consequences for misbehaviour immediately and monitor frequently.
- Enforce classroom rules consistently.
- Discipline should be appropriate to 'fit the crime', without harshness.
- Avoid ridicule and criticism.
- Avoid publicly reminding students to 'take their medicine' if on medication.

Encouragement

- Reward more than punish.
- Praise immediately any and all good behaviour.
- Change rewards if not effective in motivating behavioural change.
- Find ways to encourage the child.
- Teach the child to reward themselves. Encourage a positive self-image (e.g. 'You did very well staying in your seat today. How do you feel about that?')

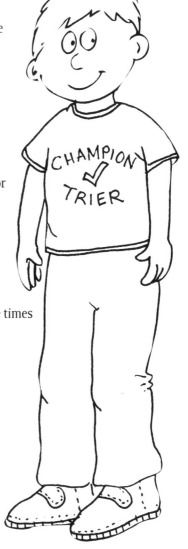

Other tips

- Private tutor and/or peer tutoring at school.
- Have classes with low student–teacher ratio where possible.
- Social skills and organisational skills training for students.
- Sports: provide individualised activities that are mildly competitive or non-competitive, like ten-pin bowling, walking, swimming, jogging, biking, karate and so on.
- Involvement in social activities like scouting, church groups or other youth organisations that help develop social skills and self-esteem.
- Allow ADHD children to play with younger children if that's where they fit in. Valuable social skills can be learnt.
- When setting homework be aware that it takes the ADHD child three times as long to complete a task at home as it would in school.

The ideal classroom

Recommendations for the learning environment

- Seat ADHD child near teacher's desk but include within the regular class seating.
- Place ADHD child up front with their back to the rest of the class to keep other children out of view.
- Surround ADHD child with good role models, preferably those seen as 'significant others'. Encourage peer tutoring and co-operative learning.
- Avoid distracting stimuli. Do not place the ADHD child near heaters, doors or windows, high traffic areas or air conditioners.
- ADHD children do not handle change well so avoid: transitions, changes in schedule, physical relocation, disruptions.
- Produce a 'stimuli-reduced area' and let all children have access to it.
- Encourage parents to set up routines for home study, including organisation of materials.

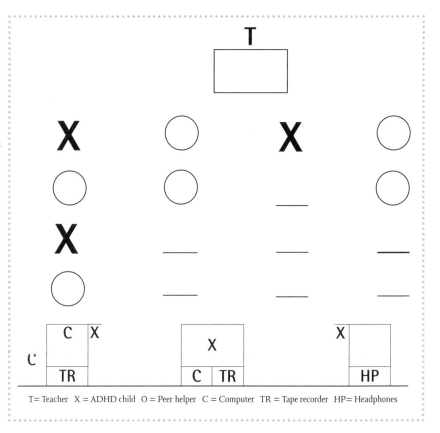

T= Teacher   X = ADHD child   O = Peer helper   C = Computer   TR = Tape recorder   HP= Headphones

Recommendations for giving instructions

- Maintain eye contact with ADHD child during verbal instruction.
- Make directions clear and concise. Be consistent with daily instructions.
- Simplify complex directions. Avoid multiple commands.
- Make sure the ADHD child comprehends before beginning the task.
- Repeat in a calm, positive manner.
- Help the ADHD child feel comfortable with seeking assistance.
- These children need more help for a longer period of time than the average child. Gradually reduce assistance.
- Ensure the child writes down daily assignments and both parents and teachers sign daily for homework tasks.

Recommendations for pupil assignments

- Give one task at a time and monitor frequently.
- Modify assignments as necessary. Develop an individualised programme.
- Make sure you are testing knowledge, not attention span.
- Give extra time for certain tasks. The ADHD child may work more slowly.
- Remember the ADHD child easily gets frustrated.
- Remember that stress, pressure and fatigue may cause loss of control and poor behaviour.

Reinforcement

Reinforcement for meeting or failing to meet expectations

Positive reinforcement

a) Praise for good behaviour/stickers/subject awards to be presented at assembly.

b) Additional privileges for evidence of consistently good behaviour.

c) Monthly honours award – recognition by head teacher.

d) Yearly award/prize day.

Negative reinforcement

a) Child is counselled by teacher one-on-one outside the classroom. This information should be communicated as soon as possible to the child's mentor. A child who is late for class without proper excuse should make up the time as specified by the teacher/mentor.

b) If the child is acting in such a way that they cannot be controlled, then one of the following should take place:

- Realignment of child seating arrangement.
- Use of private signal.
- Child should be asked to stand outside until under control.
- Child should be taken to mentor.
- Temporary revision of schedule.
- After-school detention for one or more parties.
- Exclusion from privileges and/or activities.
- Suspension (in school).
- Child sent home and parent contacted by phone.
- Parental conference.
- Good work/day card signed by teachers and parent and linked to reward system.
- A contract – attendance at community education courses, awareness and prevention course or community service.
- Suspension (out of school).
- Exclusion.

TOAD

(Talk, Out of seat, Attention, Disrupt) observation schedule

The advantages of TOAD are as follows:
○ It provides objective, baseline data for behaviour management.
○ Information is gathered at different times of the day and in different situations.
○ It enables comparisons to be made between children.
○ It can be used to measure the efficacy of interventions.
○ It can be adapted to measure individual children's difficulties.
○ It takes only ten minutes to complete(10 x one-minute observation sessions.)

Toad observation schedule

Internal	T	O	A	D
1				
2				
3				
4				
5				
6				
7				
8				
9				
10				

Name of child:_____

Age: _____

Teacher:_____

Year:_____

School:_____

Observer:_____

© Dr Sam Goldstein 1997 (reproduced with kind permission of the author)
Schedule provided as sample only. Please feel free to enlarge.

How to use TOAD

1. Carefully define the behaviours you are going to observe. You need not stick to the behaviours named in TOAD – but if you do, the author, Sam Goldstein, suggests the following:

Talking out of turn
Unsolicited spoken words directed at either the teacher (without permission) or at classmates, at inappropriate times.
Out of seat
The child is not supporting their weight on the chair when the class has been told to remain seated. Kneeling on the chair does not count as out-of-seat behaviour.
Attention
The child is not attending either to independent work or to a group activity. The child is engaged in an activity other than that which has been directed. This includes not following the teacher's directions.
Disruption
The child's actions have consequences that appear to be interrupting other children's work. These behaviours might include noise or physical contact, and may be intentional or unintentional.

2. Observe the child for one minute. When the child shows one of the behaviours you are observing put a tick in the appropriate box. After half an hour observe the child again. At the end of five hours you should have ten minutes of observations.

3. Now repeat the process in the same settings with a child whom you do not consider to have more than average behavioural problems in these areas. You can now compare the behaviour of the two children. Ideally this should be done at the same time as making the observations of the child with difficulties, in order to minimise any differences associated with the environment or with the demands of the task.

Performance checklist

Child's name: _____

Teacher's/staff member's name: _____

Date: _____

Subject: _____

Satisfactory = S

Non-satisfactory = NS

Behaviour	S	NS
Followed directions		
Addressed issues or concerns in appropriate way without interrupting a lesson		
Was respectful and co-operative to peers and members of staff		
Demonstrated a positive attitude towards peers by being supportive		
Handed in homework on time		
Punctually attended meetings with mentor		
Assessment of overall attendance and punctuality		
Comments:		

Classroom observation form

Child's name _____   Date _____   Class_____

Teacher's name _____   Headteacher's name _____

Note to teacher: Please evaluate the above-named child in each of the areas of behaviour listed below based on their performance in your class today. Use the following ratings in your evaluation:

1 = excellent   2 = good   3 = fair   4 = poor   5 = unsatisfactory

	1	2	Break	3	4	Lunch	5	6	Club
Pays attention in class									
Completes assignments									
Controls restlessness									
Demonstrates self-control									
Interacts well with others									
Follows class rules									
Concentrates on work									

Literacy and Numeracy hours

- Final 10 minutes – plenary session – whole class
- Encourage participation and questions
- Review teaching points
- Praise for good work
- Supervise students to record homework

- First 15 minutes – whole class
- Seat the ADHD child close to the teacher away from distractions
- Outline the lesson before starting
- Establish eye contact when giving instructions
- Give clear and short instructions
- Use body language to call child's attention to praise and/or reassure
- Use visuals and colour
- Differentiate questions to involve all children

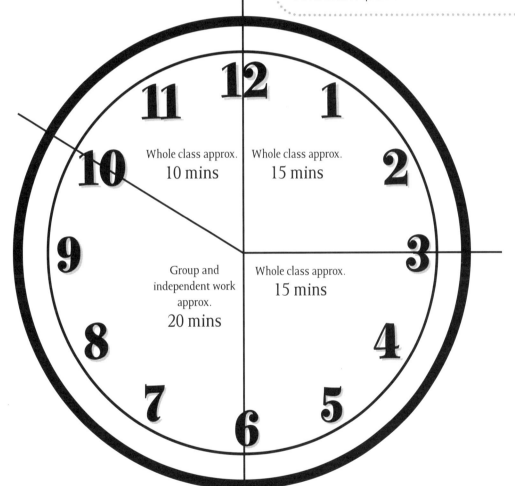

Whole class approx. 10 mins

Whole class approx. 15 mins

Group and independent work approx. 20 mins

Whole class approx. 15 mins

- 20 minutes–guided group and independent work
- Break down tasks and define the steps of the activity
- Define the time allowed/provide a timer
- Allow the use of headphones
- Assign peer helpers
- Prompt the child to start work and stay on task

- Second 15 minutes – whole class progression
- Design activities based on IEP targets
- Use multi-sensory approach, interactive teaching
- Integrate a variety of fun activities, games
- Use visuals, mnemonics, rhythm
- Reduce emphasis on competition
- Give responsibility to ADHD child to assist another peer
- Provide successful experience

Diagnostic criteria for other disorders

Hyperkinetic Disorder

1. Demonstrate abnormality of attention and activity at *home*, for the age and developmental level of the child, as evidenced by at least three of the following attention problems:
   a. Short duration to spontaneous activities
   b. Often leaving play activities unfinished
   c. Over-frequent changes between activities
   d. Undue lack of persistence at tasks set by adults
   e. Unduly high distractibility during study, e.g. homework or reading assignment

   And by at least two of the following activity problems:
   f. Continuous motor restlessness (running, jogging, etc.)
   g. Markedly excessive fidgeting or wriggling during spontaneous activities
   h. Markedly excessive activity in situations expecting relative stillness, e.g. mealtimes, travel, visiting, church
   i. Difficulty in remaining seated when required

2. Demonstrate abnormality of attention and activity at *school or nursery* (if applicable), for the age and developmental level of the child, as evidenced by at least two of the following attention problems:
   a. Undue lack of persistence at tasks
   b. Unduly high distractibility, i.e. often orientating towards extrinsic stimuli
   c. Over-frequent changes between activities when choice is allowed
   d. Excessively short duration of play activities

   And by at least two of the following activity problems:
   e. Continuous and excessive motor restlessness (running, jumping, etc.) in school
   f. Markedly excessive fidgeting and wriggling in structured situation
   g. Excessive levels of off-task activity during tasks
   h. Unduly often out of seat when required to be sitting

3. Directly observed abnormality of attention or activity. This must be excessive for the child's age and developmental level. The evidence may be any of the following:
   a. Direct observation of the criteria in 1 or 2 above, i.e. not solely the report of parent and/or teacher
   b. Observation of abnormal levels of motor activity, or off-task behaviour, or lack of persistence in activities, in a setting outside home or school (e.g. clinic or laboratory)
   c. Significant impairment of performance on psychometric test of attention

4. Does not meet criteria for pervasive developmental disorder, mania, depressive or anxiety disorder.
5. Onset before the AGE OF 6 YEARS.
6. Duration of AT LEAST 6 MONTHS.
7. IQ above 50.

Note: The research diagnosis of Hyperkinetic disorder requires the definite presence of abnormal levels of inattention and restlessness that are pervasive across situations and persistent over time, that can be demonstrated by direct observation, and that are not caused by other disorders such as autism or affective disorders.

Reprinted with kind permission from the International Classification of Diseases, The Tenth Edition (IDC 10), World Health Organisation, Geneva, 1990.

Conduct Disorder

A. A repetitive and persistent pattern of behaviour in which the basic rights of others or major age-appropriate societal norms or rules are violated, as manifested by the presence of three (or more) of the following criteria in the past 12 months, with at least one criterion present in the last 6 months:

Aggression to people and animals

1. Often bullies, threatens or intimidates others
2. Often initiates physical fights
3. Had used a weapon that can cause serious physical harm to others (e.g. bat, brick, broken bottle, knife, gun)
4. Has been physically cruel to people
5. Has been physically cruel to animals
6. Has stolen while confronting a victim (e.g. mugging, purse snatching, extortion, armed robbery)
7. Has forced someone into sexual activity

Destruction of property
8. Has deliberately engaged in fire setting with the intention of causing serious damage
9. Has deliberately destroyed others' property (other than by fire setting)

Deceitfulness or theft
10. Has broken into someone else's house, building or car
11. Often lies to obtain goods or favours or to avoid obligations (i.e. cons others)
12. Has stolen items of non-trivial value without confronting a victim (e.g. shoplifting, but without breaking and entering, forgery)

Serious violations of rules
13. Often stays out at night despite parental prohibitions, beginning before the age of 13 years
14. Has run away from home overnight at least twice while living in parental or parental surrogate home (or once without returning for a lengthy period)
15. Is often truant from school, beginning before the age of 13 years

B. The disturbance in behaviour causes clinically significant impairment of social, academic or occupational functioning

C. If the individual is age 18 years or over, criteria are not met for Antisocial Personality Disorder.

<u>Specify type based on age at onset</u>

Childhood-onset Type: onset of at least one criterion characteristic of Conduct Disorder prior to 10 years

Adolescent-onset Type: absence of any criterion characteristic of Conduct Disorder prior to age of 10 years

<u>Specify severity</u>

Mild: few if any conduct problems in excess of those required to make the diagnosis and conduct problems cause only minor harm to others

Moderate: number of conduct problems and effect on others intermediate between 'mild' and 'severe'

Severe: many conduct problems in excess of those required to make the diagnosis or conduct problems cause considerable harm to others

Reprinted with kind permission from the *Diagnostic and Statistical Manual of the American Psychiatric Association*, Washington, 1994.

Oppositional Defiant Disorder

A. A pattern of negativistic, hostile and defiant behaviour lasting at least 6 months, during which four or more of the following are present:
1. Often loses temper
2. Often argues with adults
3. Often actively defies or refuses to comply with adults' requests or rules
4. Often deliberately annoys people
5. Often blames others for their mistakes or behaviour
6. Is often touchy or easily annoyed by others
7. Is often angry or resentful
8. Is often spiteful and vindictive

Note: Consider a criterion met only if the behaviour occurs more frequently than is typically observed in individuals of comparable age and developmental level.

B. The disturbance in behaviour causes clinically significant impairment in social, academic or occupational functioning.

C. The behaviours do not occur exclusively during the course of a Psychotic or Mood Disorder.

D. Criteria are not met for Conduct Disorder, and if the individual is aged 18 years or older, criteria are not met for Antisocial Personality Disorder.

Reprinted with kind permission from the *Diagnostic and Statistical Manual of the American Psychiatric Association*, Washington, 1994.

Support groups

Groups and organisations providing support and information about ADHD include the following:

ADDA (National Attention Deficit Disorder Association)
Website http://www.add.org
A well-established US national association which provides comprehensive information.

ADD/ADHD Family Support Group UK
1a High Street, Dilton Marsh, Westbury BA13 4DL
Provides information and support for parents, adults and families affected by ADD/ADHD. Also publishes a quarterly newsletter, *Breaking Point*.

Adders.org
Website http://www.adders.org
A comprehensive website covering a wide range of information on ADHD. Adders' objective is to promote awareness of ADHD and to provide information and practical help to adults and children with the condition, and to their families.

ADHD National Alliance
209–211 City Road, EC1V 1JN
Tel 0207 608 8760
Fax 0207 608 8701
Email jim@adhdalliance.org.uk
The Alliance is not a parent support group but it seeks to act as a forum to raise awareness, exchange information and bring together all interested parties. The Alliance is a democratic parent, family and user led membership body. Free membership is offered to parents, adults and support groups.

ADDiss Information Services
PO Box 340, Edgeware HA8 9HL
Tel 020 8906 9068
Fax 020 8959 0727
Email books@addiss.co.uk
Website http://www.addiss.co.uk
Organises local and national seminars and provides information, support, training and resources on ADHD for both parents and professional workers. A large number of books and videos are for sale.

CHADD (Children and Adults with Attention Deficit/Hyperactivity Disorder)
Website http://www.chadd.org
A US national ADHD support group which provides comprehensive information, advice and support services to children, parents, adults and professional workers.

Child Psychotherapy Trust
Star House, 104–108 Grafton Road, London NW5 4BD
Tel 020 7485 5510 Helpline (Mon–Thurs 9am–5pm)
Fax 020 7284 2755
Email cpt@globalnet.co.uk
Provides a UK helpline for parents, volunteers and professional workers which gives access to a team of professional therapists with a range of specific skills in working with children and parents. Also provides information on specific emotional and behavioural problems including ADHD. The helpline operates on a maximum 50-minute call-back basis. Calls can be pre-arranged.

Contact a Family
170 Tottenham Court Road, London W1T 7HA
Tel 020 7608 8700
Fax 020 7608 8701
Website http: www.cafamily.org.uk

Henry Spink Foundation

4th Floor, 170 Tottenham Court Road, London W1T 7HA

Tel 020 7608 8789

Fax 020 7608 8790

Email info@henryspink.org

Website http://www.henryspink.org

Provides information on a range of therapies and treatments with an emphasis on alternative/complementary approaches that may prove beneficial in the treatment of ADHD.

Hyperactive Children's Support Group

71 Whyke Lane, Chichester PO19 2LD

Tel 01243 551313

Fax 01243 552019

Email hacsg@hacsg.org.uk

Website http://www.hacsg.org.uk

Provides support, information and a range of literature including *The Journal* newsletter three times a year. Also provides training and awareness-raising events at Wimbledon Branch in London (Tel 020 8946 4444).

Mental Health Foundation

20–21 Cornwall Terrace, London NW1 4QL

Tel 020 7535 7400

Fax 020 7535 7474

Email mhf@mhf.org.uk

Website http://www.mhf.org.uk

Works to meet the needs of people with mental health problems and aims to improve people's lives, reduce stigma surrounding mental health issues and promote understanding. The Foundation undertakes research and provides information (including on ADHD) for the general public and health and social care professional workers.

NARA (National Action and Research for ADHD)

Glenrosa, Lightlands Lane, Cookham SL6 9DH

Tel/Fax 01628 523 539

Email AngieT8282@aol.com

Aims to fundraise to promote and assist in furthering research into ADD/ADHD. Provides professional workers with information and research articles.

Parentline Plus

Endway House, Hadleigh SS7 2AN

Tel 0808 800 2222 Helpline

0800 783 6783 Text

Email helpline@parentlineplus.org.uk

Website http://www.parentline.co.uk

Provides emotional support for parents and families concerning ADHD. Also refers to organisations for appropriate help, advice and information about ADHD.

Young Minds

2nd Floor, 102–108 Clerkenwell Road, London EC1M 5SA

Tel 0800 018 2138 Parents' Information Service

Website http://www.youngminds.org.uk

Provides information (including ADHD), leaflets, seminars and consultancy and publishes the *Young Minds* magazine. Services are aimed at young people, parents and professional workers.

Appendix

Agnew M, Barlow S, Pascal L and Skidmore S (1996) *Get Better Grades*. London: Piccadilly Press

Barkley R (1997) *ADHD and the Nature of Self-Control*. Cleveland OH: Therapeutic Resources Company

Cooper P (1995) *Therapeutic Care in Education 4*, London

Cooper P and Ideus K (1996) *ADHD: A Practical Guide for Teachers*. London: David Fulton

Cooper P and Shea T (1999) *ADHD from the Inside: An Empirical Study of Young People's Perception of ADHD*. In: *Research Practice and Opinion*.

Canter L and Canter M (1997) *Succeeding with Difficult Students*. USA: Lee Canter Associates

Diagnostic and Statistical Manual of the American Psychiatric Association (1994) Washington: APA

Goldstein S and Mather N (1997) *Overcoming Underachieving*. USA: John Wiley and Sons.

Green C (1997) *Understanding ADHD*. Australia: Doubleday Press

Phelan T (1996) *1–2–3 Magic: Effective Discipline for Children 2–12*. USA: Child Management Incorporated

Tannock R (1999) 'ADHD: Advantages in Cognitive Neurobiological and Genetic Research.' In: *Journal of Child Psychology and Psychiatry* 39(1), 65

Train A (1995) *The Bullying Problem*. London: Souvenir Press

Further Reading

Caffrey J (1997) *First Star I See*. USA: Verbal Images Press

Canter L (1992) *Assertive Discipline*. Santa Monica CA: Canter and Associates Inc

Cooper P and O'Regan F (2001) *Educating Children with ADHD*. London: Routledge Falmer Press

Dempsey A (2000) ADHD: *Guildlines for Good Practice*. East Sussex County Council: Internal Press Document

Gordon M (1991) *ADHD/Hyperactivity: A Consumer's Guide*. New York: GSI Publications

Ingersoll B (1998) *Daredevils and Daydreamers*. New York: Doubleday Press

Kewley G (1999) *Recognition, Reality and Resolution*. UK: LAC Press

Quinn T (1988) *Grandma's Pet Wildebeest Ate My Homework*. St Louis MO: Dunvegan Publishing

Reif S (1997) *The ADHD Checklist*. Princeton NJ: Prentice Hall